TRUE GRIS

THE BEST OF ED GRISAMORE

To: Linda
Thanks for being a
loyal reader!

Ed Grisamore

Ed Grisamore
(Photography by Maryann Bates)

TRUE GRIS

THE BEST OF ED GRISAMORE

Ed Grisamore

Mercer University Press
Macon, Georgia 31210
1997

©1997
Mercer University Press
6316 Peake Road
Macon, Georgia 31210
All rights reserved.

The paper used in this publication meets the minimum requirements of
American National Standard for Permanence of Paper for Printed
Library Materials ANSI Z39.48–1984.

Library of Congress Cataloging-in-Publication Data

Grisamore, Ed.
True Gris: The Best of Ed Grisamore / Ed Grisamore.
p. cm.

CONTENTS

INTRODUCTION

A lot of love went into this book. It did not make the trip alone. There was plenty of solid advice, buoyed by the encouragement of family and friends. And, of course, there was the daily affirmation that there is no greater joy in life than writing about it.

I remember seeing a cartoon a few years ago. One guy has opened another guy's head and is looking inside. I'm not sure whether he cut it open, snapped it apart, unzipped it or simply peeled it back with his bare hands. Let's just say he was open-minded.

"Yep, there's a book in there somewhere," he says.

I've always believed I had a book in there somewhere, too. It has been rolling around inside my head, cuddling next to my heart and making its appointed rounds with my fingers whenever the words needed to come out and play.

The most difficult part is knowing when you're ready. No book is born on any one day. It is part of a process.

Whenever I've been asked when I was going to write a book, my answer always has been the same: "I work on it every day." And that is true. I never retreated to my study or holed myself up in a cabin. I wanted my first book to be the accumulation of my life's writing over the last 19 years. That's almost 7,000 days, 4,800 articles and 2.5 million words. I was ready.

The columns and stories here are the result of my work at *The Macon Telegraph*. The lone exception is "Pearl comes out of her shell," which was written my senior year at the University of Georgia in 1978, and appeared in *The Red & Black* student newspaper.

Most of my career at the Telegraph has been in the sports department, and all of it has been very rewarding.

It has taken me to 20 states and opened many doors. Over the years, I've been fortunate enough to be assigned to cover the Olympics, the Super Bowl, the Masters, four World Series and eight different college bowl games.

But the stories I have always loved best have come right out of my own back yard. Home is, and always will be, my source of strength.

In late 1996, my duties changed at the Telegraph. I left the sports department and began writing general interest features and editorial columns. I have made an effort to have some of my recent work strongly represented here.

I wish to dedicate this book to my family, and there are a lot of them, so you'll have to be patient with me. There is my wife, Delinda, and our three sons—Ed, Grant, and Jake. There wouldn't be a word in here without them. There are my parents, Dr. and Mrs. J.M. Grisamore, and my sisters Gay Hall, Susan Kasiski, Sally Davis, and brother Charles Grisamore. My in-laws, Joel and Mae Heard, have given me tremendous support, along with my grandmother, Mrs. W.E. Richards and my aunt, Mary Foster. They all are the wind beneath my wings.

I would like to thank my newspaper publisher, Carol Hudler, and editor Cecil Bentley, who have been just as excited about the book as I have been. Harriet Comer, our newspaper librarian, has always been a great help as well as a terrific sounding board for my ideas. I also wish to thank John Mitchell, who steered me to Mercer University Press and opened the door for me.

A lot of love went into *True Gris*. I expect a lot of love will come out of it.

Ed Grisamore
Macon, Georgia
July 1997

Part One

Every Day is Father's Day

Fathers need guardian angels

June 13, 1997

Fathers can't be everywhere.

As much as some of us would love to attach ourselves to every part of our children's lives, the joys of fatherhood also carry their regrets. We are not omnipresent. We need mothers and brothers and grandparents and teachers and coaches to be there for our children when we aren't.

And sometimes we need guardian angels.

At last count, I have told this story roughly 2,376 times over the past five days, so you'll have to bear with me. I have watched the look of horror invade the faces of people I have told, or heard their gasps over the telephone. It is followed by relief, then amusement.

The first thing I did Monday, the day after it happened, was call my insurance agent.

"Wayne, have I got one for you," I said. "I can guarantee you won't have another case like this for the rest of the day, week, month or even year."

Here are my headlines:

Three-year-old drives grandfather's truck down hill into tree.

Three-year-old not only is not hurt, but escapes without scratch, bump or bruise.

Tree is fine, too.

Truck is not.

My 3-year-old, Jake, is so full of wonder I sometimes call him "Amazing Jake." He has been known to put in 18-hour days without the benefit of a nap. He hasn't run off to join the circus, but he seems to be working on his resume. He's more proficient at moving around a computer mouse than some adults I know.

He is not hyperactive. I wouldn't dare call him mischievous. His mother classifies his condition as "busy." I also must point out he's at least a dozen years away from getting his driver's license.

I borrowed my father's truck last Sunday. He was going to be away for a few weeks, and he generously mailed me the key. I parked it in my driveway late Sunday afternoon and rushed off to a Little League coaches' meeting. I had not been at the ballpark more than five minutes when my wife paged me with a "911" at the end of our seven-digit phone number, so I rushed home.

You know what they say about small children. You can't turn your back on them for a second. But as they grow older, and they start learning the difference between right and wrong, a parent must search for the medium between being overprotective and careless. First you give them roots, then wings.

While Jake was playing in the driveway, my wife took something inside the house. In less than two minutes, Jake had hopped into the truck, popped it into neutral, took a roll down the hill in our back yard and parked it into a tree.

I have stood at the edge of my driveway many times this past week, looked at the tire marks in the soft dirt and run my hand across the bark of the tree that stopped his progress. My heart has probably skipped a few beats, my hands have been shaking and my voice cracks with emotion when I wonder out loud what might have happened.

The guardian angels certainly were there, maybe even the one who decided to plant that tree there many years ago. Despite the damage inflicted upon my dad's truck, had the tree not been there, the truck would have gathered more speed down the embankment and rolled into a ditch. Keep in mind that this was an unrestrained small child in the cab of a pickup.

We have asked him many times if he felt OK, and he's just as normal as ever. Not a nick on his armor, not a "boo-boo" on his body in need of a sympathy band-aid. We still aren't sure whether Jake hit the steering wheel or dashboard or ducked to the floorboard on impact. He managed to escape with only a case of bruised feelings. Of course, I hugged him so hard I probably squeezed the breath out of him.

He was most concerned that I would be angry. And that his grandfather, whom he calls "Bubba," would be mad, too. "I broke Bubba's truck," he said.

So I told him the story of a young boy who climbed into his father's car and released the emergency brake many moons ago. The car rolled backward down the driveway, hit the side of the house and knocked off the door on the passenger side. His parents weren't mad, just thankful no one was hurt. The boy's mother still talks about the vacation trip with a rope on the outside of the car door to keep her from falling out.

Of course, that knucklehead of a child grew up to be Jake's knucklehead father, so I guess it must be hereditary. If his father wasn't upset, why should Jake's dad be upset? This is a lesson of fatherhood.

4

Early Thursday morning, while the rest of the house was sleeping, I started to write this column. I heard tiptoes on the stairs. It was Jake bringing down his blanket. I wrote the rest of this column with him sitting on my lap. I know what I'm getting for Father's Day—a gift certificate from a body shop in Bolingbroke and a big hug from a lucky little boy.

Buckle up, Jake, your dad's right behind you for the ride.

Being there can make a difference

January 31, 1997

We met for the first time a few weeks before his 10th birthday. From the beginning, I could tell he was very bright, and very shy. We talked, giggled, and he tried to impress me by standing on his head.

Despite the difference in our ages, we became best buddies. We had long talks on the phone and in the car. We did neat things after school and on weekends. Fishing. Camping. Movies. Ice cream.

He was 10. I was 22. He had his life. I had mine. We shared a lot of it.

I called Andy Pilcher the other day, and he's doing just fine. He made me feel a little old, as if there already aren't enough daily reminders. He celebrated his 28th birthday three weeks ago. He no longer stands on his head, except when the computer goes down.

There are many things in my life that I'm proud of, and Andy is one of them. The shy 10-year-old grew up to graduate with honors from Central High School. He got his degree in electrical engineering from Georgia Tech. He now is a computer services specialist at the Economic Development Institute at Tech. He's married, active in his church and recently bought a new house. He even has his own home page on the Internet.

I never have tried to take credit for Andy turning out to be a well-adjusted young man. As I mentioned, he is smart as a whip. His mother, Christie, is one of the finest people I know. She taught visually impaired students in the Bibb school system and at the Georgia Academy for the Blind before moving to LaGrange.

But Andy still gives me a significant amount of credit for his upbringing. And he thanked me the other day. Again.

"I was very insecure growing up," he said. "I might have even wasted away. But being able to hang out with you exposed me to a lot of different things. It helped build my character having a male role model around who showed he cared."

Andy knows he was an at-risk kid growing up in a single-parent home. He was a startling statistic that seems to be compounded daily.

According to the U.S. Bureau of Census, almost one-third of all households that contain children are single-parent families and 61 percent of all children will spend all or part of their formative years in such an environment.

I was matched with Andy through Big Brothers/Big Sisters of Macon, and it was a blessing of good timing that I showed up on his doorstep when I did.

But even if I had not come into his life, I feel certain Andy never would have gotten mixed up with the wrong crowd or joined the equivalent of the gangs of those days. Still, there is no real way of knowing. A little preventative medicine never hurts.

I never was there to take the place of his father. I always was there to be his friend.

I grew up the oldest of five children, so I already had some big brother experience. I figured if I applied the same kind of brotherly love in this relationship with Andy, it would work. At first, I probably tried to "buy" his devotion. I was a young, single guy on a first-year reporter's salary, and I began to believe Andy might financially ruin me. Too many trips to the movies. Too many visits to the mall.

Actually, all Andy really wanted was for me to include him. I didn't have to spend money. So he would tag along when I went to a high school football game. We would go to the park near his apartment.

He would come over and spend the night on my couch, and we would stay up late watching TV. He helped me and my father build a cabin in the North Georgia mountains. I became head coach of his youth basketball team.

He remembers all of it, too.

"You sometimes let me shift gears when you were driving your car," he said. I don't remember that. He even remembers I had a blue Mercury Capri. "I still have vivid memories," he said. "I don't know if I would have gotten to do all those things if it hadn't been for you."

I was married three years after Andy and I were matched, and he served as an usher in my wedding. My wife and I still laugh every time we watch the videotape. After the reception, as we started to drive away, there was a shout in the distance. "Ed! Ed! Ed!" I rolled down the window. It was Andy. "I'll call you when you get back!"

My life changed. His life changed. I began having children of my own. He got a job. He got wheels. Soon, he did not need me as much as he once did, but we stayed in touch.

I was very proud the night of his high school graduation. I'm still proud.

There are plenty of Andys in the world who need adult role models. Big Brothers is just one agency that can help bring people together, along with other community mentoring programs. And, of course, there are other avenues, such as coaching.

This is not a plea. It's a personal example of making a difference. We talk a lot about reaching at-risk children. Simply being a friend is the best way I know how.

Norman MacEwan, author of "The Giving Tree," said: "We make a living by what we get. We make a life by what we give."

My gift to Andy was some attention and guidance.

There have been many happy returns.

Grief passes slowly through the heart of a champion

January 31, 1995

Bobby Allison pushed aside a plate of scrambled eggs and slowly pulled up from his chair.

It would be almost an hour before he would speak at the morning worship service at Pine Forest Baptist Church in Bloomfield. But a small congregation already had gathered near the church kitchen, where Allison ate a late breakfast.

A family wanted to have their picture taken with him. A young boy asked for an autograph. Finally, a man reached to shake Allison's hand. "I remember when you were racing down at Middle Georgia Raceway in Byron,'' the man said.

Allison nodded. He had flown over the old track, now abandoned, on his approach at the Macon Airport earlier Sunday morning.

Later, he would recall running late-model sportsman cars there in the late 1960s, battling Richard Petty and Cale Yarborough around the half-mile track. He remembered one race when King Richard was a no-show. Of Allison's 84 career victories, it was the only time he won when Petty wasn't in the field.

Most of the other details are fuzzy, though. Since his near-fatal wreck at Pocono in 1988, small pockets of time have escaped from his mind.

"I've got good memories of Middle Georgia Raceway. But I must admit that after the (head) injury I've lost some of my memory," Allison said. "At first, I thought I had just lost 1988. Now I see I've lost some other pieces along the way."

There are even more pieces Allison would like to forget, but he can't. They have consumed his life. At 58, he has endured more tragedy in three years than most have known in a lifetime. Racing accidents claimed the lives of his two sons, Clifford and Davey, and a close friend, Neil Bonnett.

"I have a hard time putting my losses into real words," he said softly. "I still cry a lot. Every once in a while I'll be at an event signing autographs or speaking. Somebody may show me a picture or make a comment. It may be out of the goodness of their heart, but it's still incredibly painful for me."

Allison was part of the famed "Alabama Gang"—a fraternity of racers from the blue-collar towns of Hueytown and Bessemer, near Birmingham. The gang was Allison and his brother, Donnie, and Red Farmer. Later, Clifford and Davey would follow the tail lights of their famous father.

Then Donnie wrecked at Charlotte in 1981, suffered a head injury, and never raced again. Seven years later, Bobby nearly died after a broadside at Pocono. His speech remains slowed, his memory chipped, and he walks with a limp.

The grief passes just as slowly when remembering his sons. Clifford died instantly when he hit the wall head-on while practicing for a race in Michigan in 1992. Allison was one of the first to arrive on the scene. A year later, Davey died in a helicopter crash at Talladega at the height of building a spectacular racing career. Earlier that day, Bobby and Davey had reminisced about good times. Six months later, while attempting to make a racing comeback, Bonnett smacked the wall on the fourth turn at Daytona, and he was gone, too.

"I've found there are a lot of other people in the world who have gone through tragedies and agonizing situations," Allison said. "When I speak to church groups or other activities, I try to tell them that life must go on. They must continue to do the best they can. We're taught that this life is short here on earth. The main thing is that we continue to work toward heaven."

Tears welled in Allison's eyes as he studied a lithograph designed by Macon's Johnny Goss. The scene depicts the inside of a kitchen. On a table is Davey's helmet and uniform. On the wall are photos of his sons and their racing triumphs, as well as his own.

Through a window is a scene of him working on his car and Davey riding a motorcycle. Above the garage door is a sign: "A Dream ... The Greatest Gift a Father Can Give a Son."

"You don't always have to understand why things happen," Allison said. "You just have to learn to accept them."

The heart of a champion is still there, even if it is a broken one.

Take a boy fishing

May 10, 1992

What we choose to keep in this world reveals something about our values. The personal inventory we collect is like pages in a book, each forming chapters in a human story.

I'm glad my grandfather never threw away his fishing gear.

His name was W. E. Richards, and he was 84 years old when he died last month. Although he had lived in Roswell for the past 15 years, he will be remembered for the many years he was a high school vocational agriculture teacher in Hawkinsville.

He taught countless young people how to plant a tree and fix a clutch on an old truck. On Friday nights, he helped sell tickets to Red Devil football games.

I will remember him for teaching me to fish.

My grandmother now has begun the arduous process of going through his belongings. It is sad because we miss him. Yet there are many happy memories enveloped in his keepsakes. She wanted me to have his old manual Remington typewriter and a wooden walking cane.

While visiting her a few days ago, I opened my grandfather's tool shed in the back yard. This was the kind of place where he always was in his element, tinkering with tools and planning his garden. Wherever he lived, you always could count on his basement or greenhouse being a haven of wire, wood and old parts. He didn't recycle; he restocked. He figured he could find a use for everything. And he practically could.

In a corner of the shed, I discovered two old fishing poles, his tackle box and a net. I doubt my grandfather had used them in several years. But he had kept them, and just seeing them stirred my senses.

Suddenly, I was 10 years old and standing on the banks of the small lake in my grandfather's front yard in Hawkinsville. He was teaching me how to bait a hook and blow gnats on a hot summer's day.

I almost could hear the crickets chirping from the back room at the store where he would take me to buy bait. I remembered the familiar

11

feel of a tug on the 10-pound test line, and the combination of fear and excitement that always rushed through me.

I never was entirely landlocked as a child, growing up around water no matter where my family moved. When we lived in LaGrange, my father kept his boat at nearby West Point Lake. We could see the Elizabeth River from our home in Virginia. When we lived in Jacksonville, the St. Johns River was in our backyard.

But, of all the fish I've ever caught, the ones I remember most came from my grandfather's lake in Hawkinsville. And it wasn't actually a lake. It was a pond, with a tiny island near one end. As a youngster, I imagined the opposite shore as miles away.

Years before artist Butler Brown had his paintings hanging in Jimmy Carter's White House, he looked out the window of my grandparents' home and was inspired to do an oil painting of a little boy fishing from the dock.

There's no telling how many bass, bream and catfish my grandfather pulled from lakes and streams across south Georgia. Both rods he left are well-worn steel. On one of them is a South Bend Model 550A casting reel, first manufactured in 1936.

I opened his Sears tackle box and found it stuffed with the usual bobbers and hooks, but not the kind you find today on the shelves at Wal-Mart. There were nylon-braided and catgut fishing lines. Some of the lures were made of wood and hand-painted. But I bet they still catch fish.

In one tray, I found a small tin box of split shot. It was the size of a match box, and opened in the same fashion.

On the bottom of the box was the inscription: "Take a Boy Fishing Today."

My grandfather lived those words and left behind the legacy of those words. After all, he took a boy fishing.

And now, after years of waiting for my two young sons to grow old enough to go wet a hook somewhere, I expect it's time for me to do the same.

A kid's best coach is always his father

June 19, 1993

This will be a special Father's Day for me. I recently found out I'm going to be a father again.

Our third child is on the way. By the middle of next basketball season, we either will have a complete frontcourt, an entire backfield, or a whole outfield at our house.

I'm convinced there is no greater joy than fatherhood. I'll even put it up against motherhood in a best-of-seven series. Given a choice between driving in the winning run in the World Series and being a father, the decision would be simple.

I'd want to be a dad every time.

Like anything, you have to get a feel for it. There is no instruction manual or playbook. There are so many decisions and responsibilities, but so many rewards.

A second childhood? You bet. Your athletic skills may have declined, but you never forget them. Thump a catcher's mitt or bait a hook and, all of a sudden, you're 8 years old again.

Because I love sports, and my occupation depends on it, I certainly hope my children develop the same passion. Sports are a locker stuffed with life's lessons. I think back on all that I learned from playing them and watching them. So much of it has carried over, and I find it reinforced every day.

When I was growing up, my father did not share the same enthusiasm for sports. He never played golf or went bowling. He would rather work in his garden than watch a football game on TV. To this day, he still maintains only a passing interest in athletics.

I always would grab the sports section of the newspaper first, and he would take the business pages. But he recognized my love for sports and nurtured it. He took me to high school football games and minor-league baseball games.

He did not come to see me play in Little League the summer after I finished the fifth grade. But I could forgive him. He still was in Vietnam. One of the few times I ever got upset with him was when he

13

cut off the face mask on my football helmet. He feared someone would grab it and twist me like a pretzel. So, instead of looking like Bart Starr, I looked like Red Grange.

But my father opened doors. He took me to Busch Stadium in St. Louis. We went to see the Harlem Globetrotters in Jacksonville. I saw Hoyt Wilhelm pitch in his 1,000th career game in Atlanta. My dad bought the last two tickets off a scalper so my grandfather and I could see Jerry West score his 20,000th career point for the Los Angeles Lakers in a game against the Atlanta Hawks. Dad had to sit in the car until the game was over, but he never complained.

I now feel this same sense of duty to my father's grandchildren. I want them to know how it feels to be part of a team and to appreciate watching one perform. I want them to enjoy those special moments and tuck them away. No other part of society allows us to absorb so many values while being rewarded with so many pleasures.

My oldest son has played sports for several years, and his baseball team won the league championship two weeks ago. My youngest, who soon will be a big brother himself, can't wait until next year when he starts playing. I can't wait either.

It does my heart good to see my children shooting baskets in the driveway, playing catch against the side of the house and running through the azaleas as if they were shedding would-be tacklers. I get excited when they want to watch a basketball game with me or show me their baseball card collection. Sports help create that special bond between us.

Of course, sports also have changed since I was their age. There are more athletes today, yet fewer role models. We didn't pump up our basketball shoes. There wasn't a game on TV every night. And all bats were made of wood.

But much has remain unchanged. The first nip in the air every fall makes us think football. It's still 90 feet to first base. Attitude and desire always will mean more than money. Fathers still must learn to pull their kids through without pushing them too far.

As a dad, I won't always say the right things or have all the answers. I just pray I'll be the best coach my children ever will have— on and off the field.

Advice from a dad: Keep your head up

June 18, 1994

My dad has requested something special for Father's Day. He doesn't want the usual tie or a new set of socket wrenches. He doesn't want a clever Hallmark card or even a long-distance phone call.

Instead, he has asked each of his five children to write him a letter. It's up to us what we say and how we say it. Sunday is the day when we all honor our fathers, but I've heard him whisper many times: "Every day is Father's Day."

As I've thought about what I will include in my letter, I've also thought about my own children. Should Father's Day be their gift to me or my gift to them?

So I decided to make a list of resolutions to give to my three sons— Eddie, Grant and Jake. Some of them are personal. Some are universal. Some are promises. Some are plans.

Obviously, we love sports at our house. We watch football on television and take our 7-irons down to the neighborhood park to shag balls. "Hoosiers" is one of our favorite movies. We spend what seems like most of our spring and summer at the Little League fields. So, between the diapers and homework over the next 12 months, this father resolves to honor these resolutions for his children:

• I will teach them appreciation of a new sport. It's easy to fall into the seasonal pattern of football, basketball and baseball. There's a garden variety out there to sample. Maybe we should try something different.

• I want to take them cane-pole fishing. A rod and reel are fine, but you haven't really fished until you've had bamboo in your hands and a bobber in the water.

• I will try to explain the infield fly rule. Again.

• I will beg them to choose their heroes carefully and not to be surprised if those heroes let them down.

• I will continue to teach them never to criticize an umpire or a referee. It's OK to disagree with a call, but they should avoid being critical. Enforcing the rules is the toughest task in sports.

• I will take them to a dirt-track race on a summer night, tailgating on a fall afternoon and to Augusta National on a spring morning before The Masters. Everywhere you look, you can find beauty in sports.

• I will ask them to come with me to Luther Williams Field for a Sunday matinee. I will turn them loose with some of the other kids and watch them run down foul balls behind the right-field bleachers.

• When going off to cover the Bulldogs, Tigers, Yellow Jackets, Panthers, Eagles and Hawks, I will keep sorting out the different nicknames for them. I will remind my oldest son about the time he asked me on the way to kindergarten: "Hey, Dad, which animal are you going to see today?"

• I will stress to them that they never should pay for an autograph. Athletes make millions of dollars. Children get a few dollars each week for allowance. It's not fair.

• I will espouse the virtues of my generation of athletes, just as one day I want them to tell their children about their generation.

• I will sit in the stands, keep my mouth shut and pray they never get seriously hurt.

• I will join them in admiring their trophies. But I will remind them that trophies never are as important as the memories they will take with them forever.

• I will help them understand that pitchers don't throw perfect games every time and quarterbacks don't complete every pass. The best basketball players only make half their shots. The best hitters get on base only three out of every 10 trips to the plate. I will remind them that it is just as important to learn how to lose as it is to learn how to win.

• Finally, I will teach them that there is one fundamental difference between golf and the game of life. In golf, you keep your head down and follow through. In life, you keep your head up.

Superdad and the eight Murchs

May 15, 1994

In another day and time, Bill Murchison would be just another pioneer with his wife and eight children, rolling along in their covered wagon.

His wife, Karen, would play the role of mother and school teacher. Murchison would drive the wagon and make the turn.

But this is the 1990s, and Bill Murchison is golf's bionic father. Not only does he have eight children, but the wife and kids also travel just about everywhere with him.

Tee times are coordinated with meal times, Bible study times, bath times, and bed times for Jennifer, Amy, Bill, Laura, Sarah, David, Julie and Kathleen, who range in age from 13 to 1.

"It's very important that my family be with me," he said. "I am not willing to sacrifice my family just to have a golf career."

The Murchisons are family values on a Nike shoestring budget. Murchison has won $23,917 on the Nike Tour this year, but estimates he has lost money at most events.

Why? Because it takes two connecting motel rooms and a 15-seat van (only nine miles to the gallon) to move around 10 Murchisons. That's why there always is a search for the nearest Shoney's, where kids eat free on Wednesday nights.

The family is still waiting for that first big endorsement offer, but they consider themselves rich in so many other ways. Murchison, who was winless in four years on the PGA Tour, has yet to win on the Nike Tour. But he leads the league in interviews and family portraits.

When Sports Illustrated recently profiled the family, the magazine's research department revealed Murchison had more children than 70 percent of the Nike Tour players combined. CNN and ESPN will begin filming features on the family next week. At the St. Jude's Classic last year, *The Memphis Commercial Appeal* did three stories on Murchison — and he didn't even make the field. He was first alternate.

"We feel like with all the attention we've been getting, God wants us to be a light to the world," Murchison said. "We want to be an example. We want to be an encouragement to people."

Murchison decided to take another shot at the PGA Tour in 1992 after spending eight years as a club pro in Orlando. The Murchisons already had solved the biggest issue of traveling together long before they hit the road.

"We've been home schooling for seven years," he said. Then he grinned. "Now it's more like hotel schooling."

Karen, who is a certified teacher, instructs the five oldest children in kindergarten through seventh grade. She plans the curriculum, grades the papers and doesn't cut any slack. Most school children get three months vacation during the summer. The Murchisons got just three weeks off last year.

"Whenever we go somewhere, the first question people always ask is: 'Are these all yours?' " said Karen. "I never really think about it until someone asks. To me, it's normal. Normal noise level. Normal number of people around. Then I realize it's not normal."

But then what is normal? Two? Four? Five?

"We simply see children as a gift to the world," Murchison said. "God has blessed us in eight ways. You hear people say all the time they can't afford to have more than two or three children. We've never looked at it that we couldn't afford it. If you teach, train and discipline children properly, they are a joy to be around."

Murchison finds himself in position to win in today's final round of the Nike Central Georgia Open. He trails leader Danny Briggs, who happens to have four kids of his own, by two shots. The winner gets $31,500. That's a lot of Nike tennis shoes for little feet.

While Karen and the children normally go everywhere with Murchison, they stayed at home in Acworth on Thursday and Friday while the family van was in the repair shop. They joined Murchison for his third round on Saturday and, with Super Dad in contention, plan to be there most every step of the way today.

So Murchison can be excused if he walks to every tee box waving his index finger in all directions. He's not necessarily trying to count his strokes or measure his yardage.

"Everywhere we go," he said, "we have to count heads."

Part Two

Heart of the Plate

Ed Grisamore

Finding your heart at the ballpark

March 21, 1997

The road to the ballpark is so well-traveled, my car knows the way without asking. Baseball season has arrived, and we are on automatic pilot. My wife could send me on an errand to the grocery store, and I might end up in a dugout somewhere. Out of habit.

It is exactly 4.6 miles from my front door to home plate. To get there, we ride down tree-lined streets, go over railroad tracks and past an old mill. For the next three months, our lives will be like one of those point-and-shoot cameras. We know where our focus will be.

The car is loaded with an assortment of gloves, bat bags, and buckets of balls. There is a sack of helmets, a first-aid kit, a water cooler, and what's left of the 300 pieces of bubble gum reserved for "spring training." There are times when I must be prepared with an extra set of clothes in the back seat, changing on the run between the office and ballfield.

What's that rattle? A set of worn shocks? No, it's just the aluminum bats tapping to the vibrations of the road. A sharp turn often will produce a stray baseball from the pile of equipment in the rear of the van, all 106 seams rolling across the floorboard.

Over the next 12 weeks, 20 practices and 17 games, I will manage a Little League baseball team. This is my fifth year as a coach, second as a manager. It is something I enjoy as much as anything else I do. My children have been involved in almost every youth sport this town has to offer — football, basketball, soccer, track, and golf. They all have their places, but I don't think any of them can compare to the special magic afforded by a baseball season.

It has become so much a part of my family's routine in the spring and early summer that we have withdrawal pains when it is over.

We've heard all the good-natured complaints by now, about how many folks spend so much time at the ballpark they might as well pitch a tent there. I once called a family and, naturally, got the answering

21

machine. "We're not home right now,..." the message said. "But, of course, you know where you can find us."

The ballpark isn't our second home. For the next three months, "home" will be our second home. We will smell the freshly cut grass on Saturday mornings and hear the pop of the mitt under the lights on a Wednesday night. There will be hot corners and cold suppers, but that's OK. This is the life we choose.

I have coached. My wife has been a team mother. We have two sons who have come up through the program and a 3-year-old who keeps a pile of dirt manicured behind the outfield fence. (He also is the unofficial groundskeeper, picking up every piece of trash in his path.)

My mother claims we all make her head spin. But it's like an old baseball player once said: You spend your time learning how to grip a baseball before you realize it's the other way around.

During those moments when we don't know whether we're coming or going, we have asked ourselves: Why are we doing this? Deep inside, though, we know. Two years ago, we stood on the infield dirt after the final game and almost cried because the season was over.

Said my wife: "What in the world are we going to do with ourselves for the next eight months?"

There seems to be a bond between anyone who ever has had a child in Little League, or at least a common understanding of the joy. Some of my older friends, whose children are grown, shake their heads and talk about how much they miss those days. It is a part of their past they cannot retrieve, except through the memories of old pictures and perhaps again through their grandchildren. Enjoy it while you can, they all tell me. Your children grow up, and suddenly the ballpark is just a small place on the way to somewhere else.

The season starts in 19 days. There are games to be won and lost, and hopefully some private victories along the way. Those are the ones you hope for, the ones that count the most in the end. There is the diving catch in center field, the kid who never has pitched under pressure who comes in and saves the game, the heart-to-heart talks in the dugout and the look of satisfaction dancing across a boy's eyes.

I won't forget that look. I saw it a couple of years ago on the face of an unlikely hero. I remember the sound of the bat, the ball climbing through the night air and clearing the center-field fence.

A three-run homer to win the game in the last inning. It was the stuff of dreams. His grin was as wide as the basepath he was circling. The whole team was there to hug him at home plate.

"Kirk, you will never forget this night for the rest of your life!" I told him.

And he won't.

All the answers can be found in such moments. That's why you never forget your way to the ballpark.

Your heart won't let you.

All that's left of center stage

June 27, 1993

ON THE ROAD TO CAIRO—Highway 111 turns to the south in Cairo. It winds past rich farmland toward Calvary, a town about as deep as you can go without stepping over the state line into Florida.

The directions called for us to cross four bridges, then turn left on a county road. We found the dirt road to the old Jim Sasser plantation about a mile ahead, and we drove slowly through a south Georgia thunderstorm.

I searched the cornfield on the left side of the dirt road. My friend's eyes combed the thicket on the right.

"Stop! There it is!" he shouted. I hit the brakes, and it seemed neither of us could open the car doors fast enough. The remains of the chimney were about 20 feet from the road. It was all that was left of the house where Jackie Robinson was born.

"I'm getting chill bumps," I told my friend. I suspected his heart also was racing. We found a cornerstone under some wet leaves and a few crumbled bricks on the ground. A crepe myrtle branched out near the chimney.

I tried to picture what the house must have looked like in 1919, the year Robinson was born. I tried to imagine that I now was standing on the same ground where he took his first steps as a child.

His father had been a sharecropper. His grandfather had been a slave. I stood near the fireplace that kept everyone warm that winter, when his mother gave birth to him during the Spanish Flu epidemic.

History was not made here. It was born. No other athlete this century has had such a profound social impact. Had it not been for Jackie Robinson, there might not have been a Hank Aaron or a Willie Mays or a Reggie Jackson.

I'm not quite sure why I drove nearly 180 miles in search of Robinson's birthplace. I knew there wasn't much left of it. He only lived in the house until he was 16 months old. After his father deserted the family, his mother put her five children on a train and took them to California. She hoped to free them from the shackles of a plantation

24

system that still existed in the deep South nearly a half century after slavery ended.

I guess it was curiosity that led me to the ruins of Robinson's homestead. I knew that many people in Georgia, and even some in Cairo, were unaware he was born here. There is no permanent marker in town to indicate he briefly called Cairo home.

A Pennsylvania couple once sent the local chamber of commerce a Louisville Slugger bat that Robinson had autographed. But that is pale compared to what you'll find in Royston, the home of Ty Cobb. Signs everywhere let you know the Georgia Peach was born in the northeast Georgia town. There also is a small museum.

On the outskirts of Cairo, where the nickname of the local high school team is the Syrup Makers, there is only a chimney hidden by trees on a lonely dirt road. I found it kind of sad that Robinson came and went before people here could claim him as one of their own.

When my friend and I stopped at the public library in Cairo to research Robinson's roots, we were told several unsuccessful attempts had been made to locate people who might have known the Robinson family some 70 years ago.

Although school children in Grady County still are taught that Robinson is a native son, there is no Jackie Robinson Elementary or Jackie Robinson Drive named in honor of him. We asked a young man at the library if he was aware that Robinson had been born in Cairo. Embarrassed, he looked down and said no.

So we drove nine miles in the rain to find the unmarked birthplace of a legend.

I thought a lot about Robinson while driving back to Macon. I thought about how he left that dirt road behind and blazed a trail for millions of other black athletes.

He could have been inducted into the Hall of Fame based on courage alone. But he also proved he was a superb player in his 10-year career with the Brooklyn Dodgers. He had a .311 lifetime batting average, 734 runs batted in and was a six-time All-Star. He was arguably the best defensive second baseman of his generation.

Robinson, who died in 1972, will best be remembered for his ability to endure unspeakable abuse without fighting back when he broke baseball's color barrier in 1947. Even though Joe Louis was the heavyweight champion at the time, the presence of a black athlete at the top of the boxing world did not carry the same symbol of social change that Robinson delivered as a black in the baseball arena.

A target of hatred and a victim of ignorance, Robinson must have grown weary of turning the other cheek. The most important lesson for all of us is that he never stopped turning it.

When I got home I found the words of Roger Kahn, who wrote "The Boys of Summer."

"Like a few, very few athletes, Robinson did not merely play at center stage. He was center stage; and where he walked, center stage moved with him."

But only the memory, along with a few scattered bricks, has been preserved from the place where center stage began.

It is a place that time has forgotten.

Let the tears flow, the Braves are champs

Oct. 29, 1995

ATLANTA—Is it possible to write with tears in your eyes?

The Atlanta Braves are World Series champions.

In this business, you are supposed to remain objective, suppress your feelings, wear no emotion on your sleeve.

Forgive me.

This is special. I was born in Atlanta. I am old enough to remember when they moved south from Milwaukee. I cut my teeth on the salad days of Hank Aaron, Rico Carty, and Phil Niekro. I endured the indigestion years of Biff Pocoroba and Zane Smith.

My first major disappointment as a baseball fan was when the Miracle Mets swept them out of the National League playoffs in three straight back in 1969. I can remember going to my room and crying.

These are a different kind of tears tonight.

Mark Wohlers' teammates have just mobbed him. If I could get close enough, I'd find Tom Glavine and hug him, too. Fans are dancing in the aisles. They have just finished singing "We Are the Champions of the World." They won't leave now or any time soon. I wonder if David Justice can hear them.

Sports are life's great common denominator. We put aside our differences and share the moment. Below me in their seats, total strangers are embracing. Out in the streets, cars are honking their horns. In the morning, people may wake up in Snellville and Smyrna and find pieces of Atlanta-Fulton County Stadium in their front yards.

I am having flashbacks. I watched Hoyt Wilhelm pitch his 1,000th game while I was sitting in the 30th row above the Braves dugout in 1970. I saw the Braves snap Pete Rose's 44-game hitting streak from my perch in the upper deck in center field eight years later. From my seat in the press box, I watched Francisco Cabrera single in the winning run in Game 7 against Pittsburgh in the National League Championship Series in 1992.

To me, that was the single most thrilling moment in Braves history.

Until now.

I think about all those players who have walked through the Atlanta clubhouse doors and spit in these dugouts. Some of them showed up to play in a near-empty ballpark when Chief Noc-A-Homa barely had to raise his voice to be heard. In their own way, they all contributed to this.

Different managers, front offices and fans all have passed by, like mile markers on a highway. We all had faith this highway was leading somewhere. We just didn't know when, or if, we'd ever arrive.

There are times Saturday night when I wonder if it will happen. My nerves are pounding louder than those drum beats. My nails are being chomped to the quick.

Glavine is painting a masterpiece. But, in the fourth and fifth innings, the Braves strand five runners. My gosh, fellows, end it tonight, I almost say out loud. Please.

Then, I start to feel better. Justice homers to right field in the sixth. And nobody seems to care that he had taken another kind of rip a day earlier. He criticized the low level of enthusiasm of Atlanta fans compared to what the Braves had seen in Cleveland.

He was right, of course. And wrong, too. Perhaps they were simply keeping their feelings in a check swing. After all, they've been let down too many times before. The emotional scars of having come close, then seeing it snatched away, have been slow to heal.

In the seventh inning, the Braves leave the bases loaded again. I'm not sure my heart will make it past the eighth. In the ninth, with Wohlers in for Glavine, Rafael Belliard makes a huge catch in foul territory to keep dangerous leadoff hitter Kenny Lofton off base. Now we know why Bobby Cox didn't pinch-hit for Belliard in the fourth inning with the bases loaded.

Pinch-hitter Paul Sorrento lifts one to center field, and Marquis Grissom is there to squeeze it for the second out. The Indians' last hope is Carlos Baerga, who also made the final out in Games 1 and 2.

It took forever for that ball to come down. Thank you again, Marquis. The Braves win 1-0, the same score by which they lost Game 7 of the World Series in 1991.

How long has it been? Atlanta has waited 94 seasons—30 by the Braves, 29 by the Falcons, 27 by the Hawks and eight by the old hockey Flames—for a championship by a major professional sports team.

How long has it been? The Braves played their first game in Atlanta on April 12, 1966. Two days later, Justice and Greg Maddux were born. Call it planned parenthood by the baseball gods.

The Braves now are in their clubhouse. The adrenalin is still flowing, like the champagne. Steve Avery has just come out to run the bases with a champagne bottle in his hand. He slides into home. The fans go nuts. It never hurts to have an insurance run.

I think of all the loyal Braves fans I wish could be here to share in this moment, but the stadium could not begin to hold them all. I think of friends I wish could have lived to see this finally happen. I hope my own children don't have to wait as long as I did to see it happen again.

I now know it is possible to write with tears in your eyes. I just did.

Still a kid

July 15, 1990

When Jim Tyler stands on the imaginary pitcher's mound in his driveway, he is 70 years old going on 17. He is an old man running his fingers down the seam of a young man's dream.

From the spot he has marked to the waist-high brick wall is 60 feet, 6 inches. If his aim is too high, the ball will go soaring into the back yard. If the ball caroms back too quickly, it can get by him, roll into the street and down the hill.

"Our neighbors must think it's a little weird seeing someone Jim's age out there throwing a ball in the driveway," his wife, Evelyn, said. "And anyone who goes through the neighborhood who doesn't know us must wonder what's going on."

Tyler doesn't seem to mind. Grinning like a kid, he battles the brick wall, using his slider to strike out a make-believe batter or stooping to field a hard grounder hit back to the mound. He focuses on the strike zone—the third brick from the top.

"Age is a fact of life. Old is a state of mind," he said. "My friends can't believe me. They say they couldn't throw a ball across the room without their arm falling off. I can still do most anything. Maybe not as well, or as fast, but I can still do it. I don't want to get old, laid up in a nursing home and not doing anything. I want to die a young man a long time from now."

Baseball has always been Tyler's passion. As a young boy, he can remember walking down the street, stopping after every few steps to go into his pitching windup. He once had a hat trick of three-hitters in a span of seven days at Lanier High School. He pitched in college, the Army and in semi-pro leagues across Middle Georgia. He rode the buses in Class D baseball and had a brief stint with the Class A Macon Peaches in 1951.

He was in a hurry when he pitched and won a game on the afternoon of May 4, 1946. After all, he had to run home, change clothes and go to a wedding at Mulberry Street United Methodist Church.

His own.

Obligations to his family and his dry cleaning business kept him from pursuing a major league career. But even as he grew older, and he underwent three knee operations, his enthusiasm never waned.

In 1988, he attended his first Atlanta Braves "Fantasy Baseball" camp in West Palm Beach, Fla. He was the oldest camper there. "Guys looked at me like I was the eighth wonder of the world," he said. He went back this year as the elder statesman and was voted "Best Pitcher" among the dozen hurlers in camp.

The biggest challenge of his senior citizenry came this past spring when he joined a men's 35-and-over baseball league in Atlanta. His glove, which he has had for 42 years, was older than most of the players on his team. He was 19 years older than Steve Reader of Roswell, the second-oldest player. And he was twice as old as his 34-year-old catcher, Tony Vitulli, one of two players (non-pitchers) under age 35 each team was allowed on its roster.

"When I first heard how old he was, I said: 'What? Are you kidding me? Is he going to throw underhand?'" Vitulli said. "Then, when he started warming up, I found out the man is pretty amazing. I think of my father, who is 72, and I can hardly get him to walk around the block. Jim is out there going strong for six or seven innings when it's 95 degrees."

The four-team senior baseball league played its games every Sunday at Dresden Park in Chamblee. Tyler's team, the Braves, won only three games in the recently completed 12-game season. But Tyler was the winning pitcher in two of those games and received one of the league's "Most Inspirational" awards.

Using his arsenal of fastball, slider, knuckleball, occasional curve and screwball, he started 10 of the 12 games and pitched in 70 percent of the team's total innings. Braves manager Wayne Coleman said he made only one mistake in using Tyler so extensively.

"I left him in there too long a couple of times," Coleman said. "But that's only because none of my 35- and 40-year old guys could throw as well fresh as Jim could tired. If Jim told me he was 40 years old and threw like that, I'd believe it. But, at his age, it's just unbelievable. He struck out some of the finest batters in the league. Guys would just walk away from the plate, shaking their heads in disbelief."

The league's top hitter, Ernie Johnson Jr., was one such victim. Johnson, a 33-year-old sportscaster for WTBS and the son of long-time Atlanta Braves announcer Ernie Johnson Sr., met his match against Tyler on June 10, the day after Tyler celebrated his 70th birthday.

"Ernie had been hitting me all season like he knew what was coming," Tyler said. "But I got him up there in the next-to-the-last game of the season with the bases loaded and two outs. I had a slider break off at his feet and struck him out swinging. That made my whole season."

Said Johnson: "He's a bulldog. He really bears down, and it's amazing to watch. I'm not even half his age, and he's out there running with us, challenging hitters and throwing complete games."

Tyler also had a run-scoring single in that game and finished tied for third on the team with five runs batted in. Coleman stopped the game and retrieved the ball for Tyler's keepsake — his first hit at age 70.

Although he stayed in shape during the season — swimming and throwing on alternate days — the rigors of playing soon exacted its toll.

"It sure wasn't easy leaving the house on a Monday after pitching on a Sunday," Tyler said. "I had to force myself. Sometimes it would be Thursday before I could do anything. Evelyn was always the designated driver to the games, because I was too tired to drive back from Atlanta. I'd always go right to bed after I got home. I'd sometimes wake up at night and my arm would be throbbing."

Now, the only thing that gets old are the questions. Why does he do it? How does he do it? And will he back next year?

"Unless my wife puts up too much of a howl, I'm going to play as long as I can," he said.

"Just so he's careful," Evelyn Tyler said. "At his age, and with his reflexes, I want him to be careful. But it's been great for him mentally and physically. It keeps us both young."

And if she listens carefully, she just might keep hearing the sound of that rubber ball thumping against the brick wall at the end of their driveway.

The fountain of youth must be somewhere nearby.

Heaven gets another groundskeeper

April 29, 1993

The sun was warm and there wasn't a cloud in the sky. With a slight breeze blowing to left field, the afternoon seemed to present an open invitation to play baseball.

Willie "Smokie" Glover would have approved of the day he was laid to rest.

"I always wondered why the grass was so green at Luther Williams Field," said the Rev. Arthur Reynolds. "I figured it was because Smokie knew somebody. And he did. He knew God."

When they buried Smokie Glover on Wednesday, they buried a part of Macon's rich baseball history. For 39 years, he watched over Luther Williams Field like some guardian angel. He knew the old place better than anyone.

On a perfect baseball afternoon, a crowd of more than 400 gathered at the Macon City Auditorium to pay their last respects. The eulogy was heartfelt. He was steady. He was meticulous. He was applauded for his handiwork and praised for the number of lives he touched.

His friends stood up, searching for words behind their sorrow. They said they could not think of many times when he didn't have that big, infectious grin on display. Standing over his casket, it was remembering that smile that comforted them.

"We come today not because Smokie died, but because he lived," said Reynolds. "If all of us were as dedicated as Smokie, the world would be a better place."

Said councilman Willie Hill: "We have lost a giant in this community."

Not only was Glover the groundskeeper at the second-oldest minor league stadium in the country, he was its unofficial historian. At 65, he was two years older than the ballpark with which he was so closely associated. When he was younger, he would leave his house on Walnut Street and walk down an unpaved road to the games. That same road, which forms the half-mile loop from the entrance of Central City Park to the stadium, now bears his name.

He worked for seven different baseball organizations — the Dodgers, Reds, Phillies, Tigers, Cardinals, Pirates and Braves. He kept a cap of all his former employers in his small office under the stands.

Even during the long stretches when Macon was without a professional baseball team, he would not allow the diamond at Luther Williams to fall victim to neglect.

He saw the outside of the stadium painted five different colors and the old bleachers painted four times. But those weren't the only colors he saw change. In the 1950s, he witnessed the breakdown of baseball's racial barriers both on the field and in the stands. If you asked him, he would point out two holes, now filled with concrete, in the grandstand where a pair of posts once separated the black spectators from the white spectators.

When Bob Bonifay arrived as general manager of the Macon Peaches in 1961, Glover was the first person to meet him at the gates of Luther Williams. "I got out of my car and saw this tall man with a Dodgers cap," Bonifay said. "I introduced myself, and he said: 'I'm Smokie. Welcome to Macon and welcome to Luther Williams Field.' He then took me on a tour of one of the most beautiful fields I had ever seen."

The next summer, a switch-hitting second baseman named Pete Rose would arrive at the ballpark early and help Glover groom the infield before practice. A generation later, Glover would manicure those same basepaths for a young base-stealing whiz named Vince Coleman, who swiped 145 that year in Macon (1983), a professional baseball record.

Bonifay said several major league teams expressed an interest in hiring Glover. But his roots always proved to be deeper than the outfield grass.

"He once told me: 'Chief, this is my home. My family is here,'" Bonifay said. "He said he loved Macon, and he loved Luther Williams Field."

And it was with that same love that they remembered him on an ideal day for baseball.

Smokie would have wanted it that way.

Batboy delivers in a pinch

March 25, 1995

DOUGLAS—The bat on the mantel bears his signature. The baseball cards he keeps in a drawer bear his name.

Joe Louis Reliford laughs at the thought of being one of history's most famous "replacement" players. His 15 minutes of fame have stretched into 43 years of immortality.

You can find Reliford on Pine Street in this south Georgia town, not far from the corner Taco Bell and the middle school where his wife, Gwendolyn, is a teacher.

You also can find him in the Guinness Book of World Records and Ripley's "Believe It Or Not" as the youngest person ever to play in a professional baseball game.

He was 12 years, 234 days old, and is listed right next to Satchel Paige, the oldest at 59 years, 80 days.

But it does not stop there. His photograph and a record of his achievement are on display at the Baseball Hall of Fame in Cooperstown, N.Y. The exhibit is directly across from one honoring Babe Ruth and Jackie Robinson.

He has a picture of himself standing next to the display at Cooperstown. If you look closely, you can see the tears in his eyes.

Reliford is 55 now. "The speed limit," he chuckles, drawing a one-liner on his 30-year career in law enforcement in Coffee County. He is one of this community's most respected citizens, a city commissioner and a deacon at the Pleasant Grove Baptist Church.

At a time when baseball's players and owners have given the game a black eye, Reliford prefers to keep his happy memories within arm's reach.

The night of July 19, 1952, when he pinch-hit for the Class D Fitzgerald Pioneers, did not go unnoticed by the rest of the baseball world. And it certainly changed his life forever.

The second-youngest of nine children, Reliford was named after boxer Joe Louis when he weighed in at 12 pounds at birth. It was his own fighting spirit that earned him a job as batboy for the Fitzgerald team when he was only 10 years old.

By the time he was 12, Reliford had fetched enough bats and shined enough shoes that he became a fixture in the clubhouse. He even had his own uniform. His favorite player was second baseman Charlie Ridgeway, who was named manager of the team halfway through the 1952 season. It was "Elk's Night" in Statesboro when the Pioneers played there on July 19. The stands were full, and Statesboro enjoyed a 13-0 lead in the eighth inning.

"Remember? I won't ever forget it!" Reliford said. "The crowd was hollering and restless. You know how people are when the game is lopsided. They were looking to find some other entertainment, and I was a black batboy on an all-white baseball team. I remember Charlie coming into the dugout and saying: 'If they want a show, we'll give them a show!'"

Ridgeway, who now operates radio station WBHB in Fitzgerald, remembers the crowd yelling: "Put in the batboy! Put in the batboy!"

"I never would have played him if I thought he might get embarrassed or hurt," Ridgeway said. "But I knew he was a good athlete who could play. He had hit and shagged balls with us."

In the top of the eighth, Ridgeway pulled the team's top hitter, Ray Nichting, and told Reliford—all 4-foot-11, 68 pounds of him—to grab a fungo bat.

"I thought it had to be a joke," Reliford said. "Me hitting for him? That's like sending Mark Lemke in to bat for Hank Aaron."

He took the first pitch for a strike, and lined the second into the hole between third and short. It took an outstanding play by the third baseman to throw him out by a step. In the bottom of the inning, Ridgeway handed him Nichting's glove and sent him to right field. He threw out one runner trying to advance to third base and ended Charlie Quimby's 21-game hitting streak with a catch against the outfield wall.

"The stands emptied, and they all started running toward me," Reliford said. "It scared me. I was a black batboy, and I knew I had no business out there with those white folks. I was crying. But they were there to touch me and pat me on the back. They never finished the game. When I went into the clubhouse, someone told me my back pockets were stuffed full of money."

The end came quickly, though. The publicity stunt cost Reliford his job two weeks later. The umpire, Eddie Kubick, was fired, and Ridgeway received a $50 fine and five-game suspension from the Georgia State League. They passed around the hat in Fitzgerald, taking up a collection to help pay the fine.

Reliford's small, but noble, feat has given him plenty of notoriety. He's been featured in *Sports Illustrated* and recognized by the Georgia General Assembly. He's had speaking engagements in seven states, written his autobiography and had three film studios contact him about making a movie of his life.

The young replacement player has done well.

"It still amazes me," he said. "I've got a place in the Hall of Fame. Not even Pete Rose can say that."

You might be a Braves fan if ...

Oct. 12, 1996

There are three generations of Atlanta Braves fans.

There are the neophytes of 1991 (Chipper, Javy, and Crime Dog). There are the boomers of 1982 (Horner, Murph, and Bedrock). And there are the senior citizens of 1966 (Hammer, Knucksie, and the Beeg Boy).

My friend, Jim Jones of WDEN radio, and I can count ourselves among the antiques. A few weeks ago, we started tripping down the basepaths of memory lane. Admittedly, both of us are trapped somewhere between Generation X and Generation Exit.

We're old enough to have boyhood memories of listening to West Coast games with our radios buried beneath our pillows, trying not to wake our parents. Yet we're young enough that neither of us remembers the last time the Braves met the Yankees in the World Series.

Our sentimentality recently got the best of us, and we began compiling a list of the traits of true Braves fans.

With deepest apologies to comedian Jeff Foxworthy, who has built "You Might Be a Redneck If ..." into a national act, we have collaborated on "You Might Be a Braves Fan If ..."

• Your six favorite words are: "Braves win! Braves win! Braves win!"

• You once got married at home plate.

• You saw Rick Camp's home run.

• When a nurse asks you to fill out a medical form listing any recent illnesses, you write down: "Braves Fatigue Syndrome."

• You name your firstborn son "Chipper" and your second son "Lemke."

• Even though your third child is a girl you call her "Javy."

• You rename your poodle "Crime Dog."

• You have replaced the red flag on your mailbox with a tomahawk.

• You still have your collection of popcorn boxes shaped like megaphones.

• On a history quiz, you once confused Chief Sitting Bull for Chief Noc-A-Homa.

• You know that Chief Noc-A-Homa's son was called Hit-A-Single. (Honest injun!)

• You enroll in an offseason aerobics class for the sole purpose of getting into shape for a 162-game season of tomahawk chopping.

• You send e-mail to Brother Francis on a regular basis.

• You had your first crush on "Susie the Sweeper."

• Whenever you're driving on I-285, you hold a moment of silence for Pascual Perez.

• You replaced that Butler Brown oil painting above the mantel with a picture of Sid Bream sliding across home plate.

• Ralph Garr is on your all-time Braves team.

• You follow up a friend's lament, "There will never be another Joe DiMaggio," with "There will never be another Glenn Hubbard."

• You still have nightmares about Eddie Haas.

• You once told your preacher you considered seeing Hank Aaron's 715th home run a religious experience.

• You wore any Braves apparel in public during the 17-game losing streak in 1977.

• You still have a "Wait 'Til Next Year" bumper sticker on your truck.

• You have proudly replaced it with one that reads: "Next Year is Here."

If those outfield walls could talk ...

Sept. 24, 1996

ATLANTA—It was more than a game. It was a farewell. A sellout crowd looked around Atlanta-Fulton County Stadium, took inventory of the memories and paid its last respects.

The ushers and grounds crew wore tuxedos. Not even a pre-game bomb threat could damage the spirit of this night. After all, the blasts from the past already were here. Knucksie, Geno, Felix, Sid, Murph, Clete, Road Runner, Horns, Hub, Hammer, and Beeg Boy all showed up in uniforms several sizes larger than the old days. If Pascual Perez was invited to the party, he must have been circling in traffic out on the perimeter.

The old-timers munched on ballpark hotdogs and talked about Hank Aaron's 715th home run as if it were a moment frozen in time. Ivan Allen, the mayor of Atlanta when major-league baseball made its debut here 30 years ago, threw out the first ball—again—a one-hopper to the plate.

Felipe Alou, who was the stadium's first batter in an exhibition game for the Braves in 1965, was in the visitor's dugout as manager of the Montreal Expos. In a stroke of irony, his son, Moises Alou, was Monday's final batter in the top of the ninth inning, flying out to right field. End of game.

There were fireworks and a laser show. Fans in the upper deck held up a yellow banner: "Thanks for the Memories." At Ted Turner's request, they played "Auld Lang Syne" during the seventh-inning stretch.

Oh, if those outfield walls could talk.

"There probably aren't going to be a lot of dry eyes tonight," said Ernie Johnson, the Atlanta broadcaster who was there for the Braves first regular-season game in their new stadium on April 12, 1966.

"It's probably going to affect me more than most," Johnson said. "I watched this stadium as it was being built. I used to come over here and watch them put up another bank of lights."

The lights weren't turned out forever Monday night. There will be playoff games, maybe even a World Series, on these premises. But those games will be wrapped in their own significance. There will be little time for nostalgia.

No one knows when the true end will come. That will be left up to the baseball gods. But Monday was the appropriate time to say good-bye. The Braves already had taken care of the business of clinching the division a day earlier, so it was a meaningless game cloaked in meaning.

Although Atlanta-Fulton County Stadium never has been much on looks or personality, it has been long on history. Aaron's record homer. Winning the World Series last year. Gene Garber snapping Pete Rose's 44-game hitting streak. The 13-game winning streak in 1982. Francisco Cabrera's single to score Sid Bream 10 years later to win the National League Championship Series.

And let us not forget chief Noc-A-Homa, Brother Francis, Homer the Brave, the Bleacher Creature, the ostrich races, the Great Wallenda and frog jumps. Let us not forget Walter Banks, the usher in Aisle 105 since the stadium's first dirt. Or Pearl Sandow, who never missed a home game in 24 seasons (the Braves gave her a permanent seat) until her health declined.

Built for just $18 million, it has been a bargain basement for memories. After the season, it will be dismantled, and the Braves will move next door to Turner Field. Fans soon will be parking in Horner's Corner, where Sid slid and on the spot where Noc-A-Homa used to pitch his teepee.

"It's hard to believe they're going to get the bulldozers over here," said third baseman Terry Pendleton. "I'm sure everyone will be kind of caught up in the new stadium. But they'll also look across the street, and there will be an awful lot of memories left over here."

Tom Glavine certainly has his own chapter in those memories. He won a Cy Young pitching in the Launching Pad. He shut out Cleveland in the clutch to nail down the World Series and bring Atlanta its first major professional sports championship.

"This stadium has seen some great things, but not just from this era," Glavine said. "Those memories jump out at you a little more because they're recent. It makes me a little sad to see this place go because it's special. But it's the price of progress, I guess. We've seen the end of the Boston Garden and Montreal Forum."

Part of you realizes we live in a disposable society. We concede the new stadium will be ninefold better, yet we want to cling to this sacred ground like sentimental fools. Some of us grew up here, tagging along as Atlanta matured as a professional sports city.

But the other part wishes you could preserve history and recycle the old ballyard as if it were an organ donor. The entrepreneurs already are taking orders on the infield dirt. Invest in your clump of soil now.

"I'd like to take home plate, but I forgot my shovel," said Bream, laughing.

"Left field is mine," said Rico Carty. "That's where the greatest fans in the world were. I can still hear them calling my name: 'Rico! Rico! Rico!' It makes me wish I was still playing again."

Aaron wants his old locker, the one that has been sealed inside the Braves clubhouse. Niekro has put in a request for two wooden seats.

"I can't think of a better way to see the sun come up and go down than sitting in one of those wooden seats in my backyard, drinking a cup of coffee," Niekro said.

Then he reflected: "I'm sad to see it end. This place is going to be tough to replace."

Amen.

Part Three

Searching for the Write Stuff

Words are what really matter

May 23, 1997

I spend most of my time asking questions. It's part of my job.

But this was one of those occasions when I was summoned to provide an answer. Emily Walker had asked if I would speak at Tattnall Square Academy's 17th annual "Senior Capstone." It was a special opportunity to address a group of young people who were graduating from high school and ready to become students of the world.

There were six speakers on the program—a rabbi, financial planner, assistant district attorney, hospital administrator, priest, and myself. There was a challenge here, too. We would be "preaching" from the pulpit of Tattnall Square Baptist Church.

"This year's theme is: What Matters," said Emily, a senior and Tattnall's student council president. "The rest is up to you."

I thought about a lot of things that really matter. Family. Faith. Careers. Education. Health. It was interesting to hear the other speakers who went before me.

Rabbi Uri Goren listed 10 rules for a human being. Bruce Farman emphasized that what we want to do in life is not as important as what we want to be. Michael Gilstrap urged the seniors to make a contribution to the world, not live off it. Robin Flanders, a member of Tattnall's first graduating class in 1974, talked about making a difference, even if it was something as simple as planting a shade tree for future generations to enjoy. Father John Cuddy said what matters can be something as seemingly insignificant as a battery, like the one in his hearing aid that recently quit on him while he was watching a movie.

What "mattered" to me was what draws everything together in our lives.

Words.

I asked Tattnall's seniors if they could remember, or had been told, the first word they ever said. Mine was "boat." My grandfather kept his by the lake near his house in Hawkinsville. It must have made a huge impression on me, just as other words have in my life.

I know my first word, but I'm not sure what my last will be. Of course, I hope it doesn't come for a long, long time. If I die suddenly, without warning, I won't have the chance to choose how I deliver my last breath.

But what really matters are the words we use in between. They are the most important tools we have here on earth. What we say, what we write, and what we read determine who we are and what we become.

Words shape the way we see the world. Words reinforce the world we see. They give it strength. They give it meaning. They open and close doors. Can you imagine living a day of your life without words? Rudyard Kipling once called words "the most powerful drug used by mankind."

I told these seniors that their whole lives will be formed by words—nouns, verbs, adjectives and dangling participles—everything they dreaded learning in English class.

Wherever you go, whatever you choose to do, and whoever you choose to be with, words will follow you there. You must learn what they mean and what to do with them. I told them Mark Twain once said the "difference between the right word and the almost right word is the difference between lightning and a lightning bug."

Obviously, words are an important part of my life. I have written almost 2.5 million of them.

Some have been big words, some small. Some have inspired, others agitated. I have had my words framed and laminated, sealed and delivered to other towns and states, faxed, e-mailed, tucked away in drawers and tacked to the refrigerator door. (Refrigerator doors are the highest honor afforded any journalist.)

I also know I've been burned, shredded and recycled. While at the Museum of Arts and Sciences, I once saw my column lining the bottom of a chinchilla cage. That's fairly humbling.

There are words I'm glad I wrote, especially if they have lived on in someone's head or heart. There are words I'm glad I read or heard. All of us have been influenced by a line in a book, a movie, a song. There are words I'm glad I said. I can think of two important words I said to an important person in my life on a July afternoon 15 years ago. Those words were: "I do."

Then I left these seniors with some words about words, by Gene Griessman. I have them on a wall above my desk.

"Well-chosen words can enable you to rise to heights you may now only dream of. Words can paint dreams, correct errors, and pass along truths to the latest generation. Words can interpret the present and speak to the future. Words can stir up the worst or find the best, destroy or build up, tarnish or cleanse. Build up your knowledge so that your words are true. Nurture your

spirit so that your words are kind, strong and wise. Words, once they are released, take on a life of their own and find lodging in places and hearts that you may never know. But after many days, they may return to haunt or bless you. Think carefully before you let them go."

In the end, you can only hope your words have made a difference.

Maybe this time, they did.

Macon's own Sign-feld

Dec. 10, 1996

The words go up. The words come down. Bob Berg isn't always sure how they will work. Or if they will work at all.

Need some advice? "Eat Here," begs the sign outside Sid's Sandwich Shop. "The wife you save may be your own." Got a growl in that stomach? Never fear, says Sid's sassy sign. "Our breads are bundles from leaven." Dry spot in the back of your throat? That's a sure sign of thirst. "Seven days without our tea makes one weak."

And then there is the food for thought. At Sid's, the marquee asks: "Why isn't phonetic spelled the way it sounds?"

Since he began posting clever and entertaining messages outside his Forsyth Street sandwich shop 12 years ago, Berg has become a letter laureate. Just call him Macon's Sign-feld, a ham-and-cheese wordsmith on wry.

There are times when he tries to be funny. Other times, he's simply attempting to editorialize and make sense of a crazy world.

"Even though the menu stays the same, the sign changes," said Berg. "It has taken on a life of its own. Anybody can put up a sign to advertise a lunch special. There is so much traffic on this street, why not put up happy messages, even if they have nothing to do with the business?"

His creativity once sold a truck. "Roast Beef Sandwich: $2,800. Get a truck free." He struck a few funny bones during the 1994 Winter Olympics when the sign announced a "Tonya Harding Special — Club Sandwich." Other times, the sign just plain perplexes: "There are three kinds of people. Those who can count and those who can't."

"Most of the time, the messages are a little off-the-wall," Berg said. "I've had some young employees over the years that popped ideas into my head. Customers come in and make their own contributions. Sometimes, there's almost this pressure to come up with something witty all the time."

Old Sid would be proud. Macon-born poet Sidney Lanier, after whom Berg's two sandwich shops are named, never had to put up the sign "Hey, Buddy, can you spare a rhyme?" as once Berg did.

Chances are, he would agree with Berg's word prowess. "Why is abbreviation such a long word?" a Sid's sign asked. That, of course, was later followed by some grammatical advice: "Don't use a big word when a diminutive one will suffice."

When Berg and his wife, Bess, opened the original Sid's sandwich site downtown 15 years ago, they had no problem coming up with the original name. After all, Lanier, along with his father and uncle, all had practiced law in the building at 336 Second Street in the 1870s.

The name not only was literary, it was alliterative. "It made sense because of all the S's," Berg said. "Sid's Sandwich Shop. Soups. Salads. And we were located on Second Street."

Admittedly, Berg doesn't always manage to dot every "i" or cross every "t." When he advertised a "Honeymoon Salad: Lettuce Alone," you could hear the chuckles all the way over on Georgia Avenue. Then a customer came in and wanted to order one. "I was embarrassed when I had to explain to him the sign was just a joke," Berg said.

Berg is not exactly non-partisan. His "political special" was a bologna sandwich—hold the bread. His major regret came a few years ago, when President Clinton's approval rating dipped to an all-time low. Berg tossed Clinton's name onto the sign along with a Bible verse, Psalms 109:8. "Let his days be few; and let another take his office."

There were two things Berg didn't realize after the sign went up on a Saturday night. First, everyone passing by on their way to church the next morning had their Bibles handy on the front seat. The other was that Psalms 109:9 follows with: "Let his children be fatherless; and his wife a widow."

As they say in the food business, that was not a sign of good taste. Says Berg, shaking his head: "A big, big mistake." It also was the most short-lived sign in Sid's history.

So Sid's now sticks to its bread-and-butter, which is getting the most out of a two-sided sign on a one-way street. Berg once placed "God Bless You" on the back of the sign, but evidently someone did more than just steal a glance in their rear-view mirror. A thief stole the 11 letters.

Still, you can't steal the spirit of the messages. After all, as the sign once boasted, "We can't tune a piano, but we can tuna fish."

Sid's can hardly wait for the first real cold snap of the season, a day when it's so cold the lawyers have their hands in their *own* pockets.

The sign will be there, waiting for that one.

Books that go thump in the night

February 23, 1997

We practice the three B's at our house every night. Bath. Books. Bed. Maybe I should say my wife and I *try* to practice the three B's with our three children.

The nightly routine does not always go like clockwork. Even at a young age, our boys have developed a fundamental skill. It's called stalling.

As much as we love them, there also is real joy in getting them to go to bed. It gives us a chance to finally sit back and relax, to talk and catch up, maybe watch the evening news.

Sometimes, though, we hear things that go thump in the night.

10:30 p.m. Thump.

10:50 p.m. Thump.

11:10 p.m. Thump.

It is not the noise of a branch scraping the roof or a furnace in need of repair. It is the sound of books hitting the floor, one by one. Our 9-year-old son, Grant, who usually crawls into bed with as many as a dozen books, will drop them as he finishes.

I guess we could dash up the stairs, turn out his light and threaten him by unleashing all those parental powers of restriction. "You should have been asleep long ago," I sometimes will warn him.

Most of the time, though, my wife and I just look at each other and grin when we hear the plop of pages coming from the upstairs bedroom.

There is plenty of satisfaction in knowing that, although your child may not be closing his eyes, at least he is expanding his mind. He often falls asleep with his face still buried inside a book.

I am convinced that Grant has become an avid reader because we read to him constantly when he was younger. We did it with his older brother. We are doing it with his younger brother.

We believe in reading to our children. We may not always buy them everything they want at the toy store. And we refuse to succumb to a happy meal every time we are in the vicinity of the golden arches.

But I made a pledge when I became a father. If my child asks me to read him a book, I will not turn him down. I don't care where we are or what we are doing, I never will allow myself to be too busy or too tired to snuggle up and read.

There has been a lot of discussion about our American educational system. We want to redefine it. We want to build new schools to enhance learning. We want to change the curriculum because it has not produced significant results.

Actually, a better solution to raising smarter children who are responsible and resourceful can be found in a book. Any book. So long as it is read.

Ruth Love, superintendent of the Chicago Public School System in the early 1980s, said it best: "If we would get our parents to read to their preschool children 15 minutes a day, we could revolutionize the schools."

I feel a sense of duty to read to my children because my mother read to me. Some of my strongest childhood memories involve her reading to my sisters, brother and me. Those were the days before cable TV and VCRs.

She helped us find our own window to the world. And when Strickland Gillilan wrote "The Reading Mother" in the book, "Best Loved Poems of the American People," he probably had my mother in mind.

> *"You may have tangible wealth untold.*
> *Caskets of jewels and coffers of gold.*
> *Richer than I you can never be*
> *I had a Mother who read to me."*

My mother recently told me she was pleased that I still remember the books we read, many of them during the year my father was in Vietnam.

"It was not always easy, but I think the most important thing is that we were together, loved, warm and cozy and entertained," she said. "The reader has just as many blessings as the listener. We read 'The Little Lame Prince' on my big poster bed when we lived in Virginia. We also read 'Charlotte's Web,' 'Charlie and the Chocolate Factory,' 'James and the Giant Peach' and 'Pippi Longstockings' long before they were made into movies. We read 'Puddin' Head Wilson' (by Mark Twain) and 'True Grit' on the porch in Jacksonville."

My mother still is one of the most prolific readers I know. She always has a "good book going," and usually two or three at the same time. She also never misses an opportunity to recite a page or chapter out of a book to anyone who will listen.

If you have children, grandchildren or know of any children you can read to, I would encourage it. My mother, who once heard the same thump of books hitting my bedroom floor, says her favorite book now is "Simple Abundance," a daybook of inspiration by Sarah Ban Breathnach.

"Most of us long to experience Paradise on earth. People who read do," Breathnach writes. "Whoever said that you can't take it with you obviously never read a good book. For everything you've ever read, loved, and remembered is now a part of your consciousness. What is once cherished can never perish."

Books are a lot like children. You love them. Forever.

Spellbound sign still a wiener

June 20, 1997

Hardly a day goes by that Spyros Dermatas doesn't get offered a spelling lesson.

Someone will drop by his family-owned business on Cotton Avenue or one of the six other Nu-Ways scattered across Macon from Bloomfield to Baconsfield. They will order a hot dog and relish the idea of making a correction on the sign out front.

"Hey, don't you know that's not the way to spell wiener?" they will say, pointing out the error that is printed on everything from the napkins to the paper sacks.

The question can get as stale as a three-day-old bun. Dermatas just nods and smiles.

"You don't have to remind me," he will say. "I learned it is 'i before e, except after c' back at T.D. Tinsley Elementary."

But you don't mess with tradition. That's why when the colorful neon sign arrived at 430 Cotton Avenue with what appeared to be a typographical error 60 years ago, it stayed that way and has become somewhat of a downtown landmark.

"Best Weiner In Town ... Nu-Way Weiner Stand."

Yep, that's weiner, not wiener, and a double dog of it. What's next? Hot dawgs?

But according to Dermatas, the intentional misspelling is nothing nu, er, new.

His great uncle, James Mallis, immigrated here from Greece (not Grease) and opened Macon's first fast-food restaurant at its present location in 1916. He wanted a snappy name, thus the "Nu Way."

"The name was on the glass window and door, and wiener was spelled correctly for the first 21 years," Dermatas said.

But when two of his other uncles, George and Harry Andros, purchased a neon sign in 1937, they wanted more than just a marquee.

"They wanted something catchy to draw people in, so they decided to misspell wiener," Dermatas said. "It's always been a conversation piece. When somebody sees it on the menu for the first time, they might mention it. So we have to tell them THAT'S THE WAY WE SPELL IT!"

Of course, others have intentionally and unintentionally tried to steer the big weenie down the path of grammatical rehabilitation. It has been identified as Nu-Way Wieners on billing statements and reference material. A local artist recently sent Dermatas a cross-stitch pattern she had made of the Cotton Avenue Nu-Way for his approval. Dermatas told her everything looked great except that she needed to correct the "e" before "i" on a Nu-Way.

I can sympathize with the Nu-Wayvers. I've seen my last name spelled about 23 different ways. At one time in my life, I've been a Grissamore, Grimore, Grizmore, Grimamore and Gritsmore. I'm certainly used to it by now. More often, I'm surprised when someone spells it correctly the first time or without asking.

It's not an easy name. It's the only one in the phone book, in fact the only one in any phone book within a hundred miles of here. (If there happens to be an Ed Grimamore down Abbeville, I'm getting your mail.) My mother's maiden name is Smith, probably the most common last name in the country. Go figure!

I'm not over-sensitive to misspellings, just aware of them. After all, I am in the "word" business. Still, I don't cringe every time I pass a Nu-Way Weiner, although my high school English teacher probably would get out her red pen.

I don't pull over to protest the corner Kwik Way Food Store or the La-Z-Boy Showcase. I don't try to correct my sister, who is an extremely lousy speller, because I am just thankful that she takes the time to e-mail me a letter from London every morning. I once received an engraved trophy of appreciation from a local basketball team that called me "supeoriror." Hey, it's the thought that counts.

When I was in the fifth grade—in the days before computers and when mothers were your only spell checkers—I did a report on Portugal. Only I did the entire report, cover page and all, and spelled it "Portugual" all the way through. Thank goodness for Clorox, which works about the same as corrector fluid. To this day, I've never again misspelled Portugal.

People have stopped to ask me, several times recently in fact, "Don't you have anybody down at the newspaper who can spell?" As a matter of fact, we do. Lots of them. But mistakes do creep into copy. (My theory is that sometimes the gremlins come out late at night, after we've already put the next day's edition to bed.)

It's even been suggested that the paper hire Cody Boisclair, the 14-year-old from Warner Robins who finished fourth in the National Spelling Bee in Washington, D.C., as a proof-reader.

Look around. Bad spelling has almost become permissible in our society. It's on signs. It's in advertising. Is it laziness or a sign of the times? You know the old battle cry: "Bad spellers of the world, untie!"

Remember when former Vice President Dan Quayle tried to correct the spelling of the word "potato" at a New Jersey elementary school spelling bee a few years back? He tried to add an "e" and it became a national issue that the VP couldn't SP.

Quayle ignored Shakespeare ("To bee or not to bee!") and quoted Twain: "Never trust a man who has only one way to spell a word."

Sounds like a weiner to me.

Part Four

When You Figure It Out, Please Page Me

Questions in search of answers

March 28, 1997

You finally reach a point in your life when you realize you no longer know it all. This revelation comes with a certain sense of resignation, for you have gone from a person who thinks he knows everything to one who is overwhelmed by it.

I don't know when you're supposed to assume you've arrived, just that I'm already there. Maybe taking the SAT was the first clue. Or maybe it was the time the lady from the Gallup poll called and started asking my opinion on subjects I did not know. Maybe it came from watching too many episodes of "Jeopardy."

Or maybe it simply was when I found myself with a house full of kids. They always ask the rhetorical question: "But why not?" I have developed the vague, rhetorical answer: "Because I said so." (I have since learned that parents pass down this answer from generation to generation.)

So I started keeping a list, partly for my own information, but mostly to save my own strength. I have stopped pretending to be a know-it-all and started conceding that I know only a fraction of what I should.

Here are 37 questions and zero answers. Don't worry. There are more where these came from.

1. Why is it that I can turn on the radio and hear a song I have not thought about in 20 years and remember every word, yet I can't remember what I had for breakfast this morning?

2. Is there a black hole for socks in the laundry room?

3. How does the reversible center lane change on Vineville Avenue, and what do you do if you're in it when it switches over?

4. Why are the flashlight batteries always dead?

5. Why is it that so many doctors consider their time more important than your own?

6. How did Bill Clinton get re-elected?

7. Where is the remote?

8. Do people really believe they're going to win the lottery?

9. Why do we drive on parkways and park on driveways?

10. Is there any redeeming value to drinking caffeine-free Diet Coke?

11. How can something as tiny as pollen knock you off your feet?

12. Are all those young people with mega-bass stereos trying to blow up their cars? (Sure sounds like it.)

13. Why is it so difficult to get grass to grow in some parts of your yard yet it will come up through the cracks in the sidewalk?

14. Why is it that I can sit down with 50 available cable channels in front of me and can't find anything worth watching?

15. Why do you see people holding "Will Work for Food" signs less than 100 yards from a fast-food restaurant with a "Help Wanted" sign out front?

16. Why is it that they say a prayer before Bibb County school board meetings but students are not allowed to pray in schools?

17. Where do they get those people on daytime talk shows?

18. Why is it that when something is sent by car, it is called a shipment but when it is sent by ship, it is called cargo?

19. Exactly who is this "Bubba" guy and where does he live?

20. Why does the "other" checkout lane at the supermarket always move faster?

21. Why is it impossible to watch a movie in a theater without eating popcorn?

22. Why do we sing "Take Me Out to the Ballgame" when we're already there?

23. Why, pray tell, has the song "YMCA" survived?

24. If con is the opposite of pro, is Congress the opposite of progress?

25. Why is it so tough to get your children out of bed and ready for school during the week, but on weekends they are up with the dawn's early light, waking you to ask you to go get doughnuts?

26. Why do fat chance and slim chance mean the same thing?

27. Why are there interstate highways in Hawaii?

28. Why is "abbreviation" a long word and "long" a short one?

29. Why do hot dog buns come in packs of eight and 12, but Oscar-Mayer wieners come in packs of 10?

30. Who are the "they" in "You know what *they* always say"?

31. Is the glass half-empty, half-full or simply larger than it needs to be?

32. How old will we all be when they finally finish widening Northside Drive?

33. Why do baseball managers wear the same uniforms as the players, but football and basketball coaches do not?

34. What is another word for thesaurus?

35. If Dennis Rodman did not exist, would we have to create him?

36. Why is it that when you get your coffee just the way you like it, the waitress comes by and "warms it up"?

37. What exactly is a Whoopee?

Life on the mourning bench

Dec. 3, 1996

Don Woodall and Lester Dykes sat outside Belk Matthews, waiting for their wives to come up for air.

"We call this our mourning bench," said Woodall. "They're in there shopping. We're out here mourning."

It is said that misery loves company, which I guess is why you find so many men riding the benches at Macon Mall these days. 'Tis the season.

Trying to keep pace with your shop-happy "significant other" can siphon your energy. Sometimes, you must wander off in search of support groups. Just ask Woodall and Dykes, who both live in Cochran.

"There are mourning benches all over the mall," said Woodall, who wasn't really mourning. He was laughing, despite making his third trip with his wife to the mall in the past week.

Men don't necessarily have an aversion to shopping with women, just a different approach.

"I make up my mind what I'm going to get before I leave home," said Dykes. "When I get to the store, I go straight to it."

The wives, however, operate by a different procedure. The joy of the hunt is not in the kill, but the quest.

"She doesn't always buy, but she looks, looks and looks," said Woodall. "What bothers me is standing at the same clothes rack for 30 minutes while I'm waiting."

I can relate. I'm convinced there is nothing more physically and mentally draining than shopping with your wife. I can say this after recently being drop-kicked through the mall.

Tell me. Why do I have the stamina to put in long hours at the office, but can't last 45 minutes at Macy's? I exercise at the Macon Health Club four days a week, keep up with three active children at home and have twice played in 100-hole golf marathons. But that's no guarantee I have the endurance to make it from J.C. Penney to Sears.

As one of my colleagues said: "It's a whole different set of muscles."

62

Maybe it's not so much the length but the depth. There's no such thing as a straight line from one department to the next. There are hazards, traps and lures. One must have deep pockets to survive the obstacle course.

Before I chew a little shoe leather here—purchased at the mall, of course—let me back off. I'm not trying to stereotype wives, girlfriends or any shopping enthusiast who can recite the battle cry: Veni, Vidi, Visa (I came. I saw. I charged it.)

But I do know that my wife, Delinda, often plans family vacations around their proximity to outlet malls. This is a woman who can sleep through three doze buttons on the mornings she has to work, yet will leap out of bed the day after Thanksgiving so she can be there for her annual sunrise service at the mall.

Evidently, she was up too early to see the front-page story last Friday. A consumer advocacy group proposed a "Buy Nothing Day." In her mind, and millions of others, the traditional after-Thanksgiving sale is a "Hold Nothing Back Day."

I'll forgive her. Most of time, she laughs at my shopping jokes— "Custer wore an Arrow shirt" and "Did you know that Tommy Hilfiger is starting a new line of extra-large shirts called Tommy Fullfigure?"

But I'm convinced most of her amusement comes from watching me drop while she shops. Having me tag along is her own form of torture, and there are times when I have no choice but to go with her.

I asked Ben White, a friend who is a family therapist, if there was a psychological term for this condition. Or, better yet, a treatment. Unfortunately for Ben, he's been afflicted for 30 years while shopping with his wife, Peggy.

"I think I'm like most men," he said. "I want to get in and out of a store as quickly as possible. If I can't find it, I go on. But women always have a Plan B and Plan C."

White also said females don't understand why males feel compelled to sit in a deer stand all morning any more than we understand their need to participate in every "one day only" sale in store history.

"For many of them, shopping is really their sport," he said. "They get in a competitive mode."

My antidote is to administer multiple doses of mild agitation, impatience and boredom. My wife simply calls it "hovering."

Hovering requires years of practice, circling while looking at your watch. A few years ago, I was hovering at Saks Fifth Avenue in Atlanta, when she accused me of Saks-ual harassment.

Most of the time, though, I concede. "Get thee to a bookstore," is her usual command. So I disappear. I might as well go browse for a book.

Usually, there aren't enough empty seats on the mourning benches.

Admissions of a UGA-ly graduate

April 19, 1997

The late Dean William Tate always issued two qualifications for admission to the University of Georgia. If you were "breathing and grew up with red dirt between your toes" then Tate believed it was your birthright to matriculate in Athens.

I'm a Georgia graduate, and we used to joke there were only two requirements on the admissions application—a geography and medical exam. One, you had to live in the state. And, two, you had to have a pulse.

I tried not to judge some of my free-spirited and academically challenged classmates during my years at UGA, no matter how many times I wondered what they were doing in college except spending their parents' money. I know that some of the brightest minds and deepest thinkers in this state were routed through Athens for their college education. It's just that, traditionally, the admission standards have been pretty UGA-ly.

That's why Georgia Tech graduates have deployed a few jokes at the expense of their UGA neighbors, especially the one about the college president claiming he wanted a university the football team could be proud of.

John Albright, senior associate director for admissions at Georgia, laughs at most of the jokes, though he admits they are getting old. He said Stephen Portch, chancellor of the university system of Georgia, even told a joke at a chamber of commerce meeting in Watkinsville.

"Tech and Georgia once were recruiting the same high school football player. The Tech coach went to the player's home and saw a calculus book on the table," Albright said. "The Tech coach said: 'You're our kind of player. What do you think of that calculus?' The player said: 'Oh, that's not my book. The Georgia coach brought it and said if I went to Tech I'd have to use it.'"

But the reality of the calculus joke no longer fits the equation.

"We teach calculus to a lot of people here, too," Albright said. "And we have a lot of people who already have had it in high school. So the joke doesn't ring true like it once did."

What blows my mind, which never had to deal with calculus, is that it suddenly has become very, very difficult to get into Georgia. For a number of Bulldog wanna-bes, UGA has taken on a new meaning: Unlikely Getting Admitted.

The university received some 12,000 applications for a record 4,100 spots in its freshmen class for next fall. It was even more combative last year, when there were 13,000 scrambling for 3,500 spots. Only about two-thirds of each number were accepted, and approximately one-third enrolled. This year, only applicants with a grade-point average of 3.5 or better and at least an 1150 on the SAT could feel relatively secure about their chances.

I had classmates who couldn't make 1150 on the SAT if they added up their two attempts. But that was then, and this is now.

"When I first started working here (in the admissions office) in 1979, I had to explain to people there was such a thing as an honors program at UGA. There were opportunities, not just for good students, but for really good students," said Albright. "That was a new concept for a lot of people. Now, we don't have to introduce that concept. People know we're good."

The state's largest public university is in the middle of an admissions revolution, and trying to keep up with supply and demand. Just 12 years after the scandals of the Jan Kemp era, it has become a tough ticket. Make that a Lotto ticket.

At least part of the hefty competition has been fueled by the lottery-funded HOPE scholarship program, which offers full tuition at state colleges to high school students who graduate with a "B" average or better. Now students who might have taken their quest for higher learning outside the state's borders are staying put.

It may not exactly be the Ivy League, but it no longer is being brushed off as the Kudzu League, either. "It's a fact of admissions life that you also are known by the company you *DON'T* keep," Albright said. "When you start turning down relatively good students, more students decide they want to come."

The backlash of the boom has been that UGA legacies and fourth-generation Dogs are being turned away. This has produced a combination of anger and bewilderment. The university has tried to rectify the overwhelming demand by reducing the number of out-of-state admissions from about 16-18 percent to 11 percent. Enrollment has been capped at 30,000.

"We've maxed out in our capacity to take on more students," Albright said. "It's not a housing issue. It's a classroom issue. ... We have to ask if we want to keep growing so that the same proportion of students can still get in. At what point does the education change when we have 45,000 to 50,000 students in Athens? We want to be accessible without becoming Harvard. We don't need a Harvard in Athens.

"And, at the same time we're starting to sound more and more elite, there still is a culture that says we're a part of this state. We don't want to become another Virginia, which has become so exclusive that it almost separates itself as a state school.

"Sure, 'How 'Bout Them Dawgs' is poor grammar, but it's also enthusiasm. And it's also an outward and visible sign of connection to every person in this state."

If you're a Georgia alum, that red dirt between your toes is now paydirt. The value of your degree is going up. Just think, one day I will tell my grandkids I went to Georgia and they will say: "Gee, Gramps, you must have been really smart!"

Guess I was. Even without calculus.

This one's a keeper

September 3, 1994

You may not believe this story.

Three Cochran men have had to rub their eyes, swear on a stack of Bibles and do everything short of taking a lie-detector test to convince folks that it actually did.

"I'd have a hard time making up something like this," said Jerry Towns. "Still, I keep waiting for those guys with the white coats to come after me with a strait jacket."

Golf and fishing have produced some of the greatest lies known to mankind. What's the old golf saying? It's a game where the balls lie poorly and the players lie well.

This golf tale/fish tail began on a late August afternoon at The Woods Golf Course in Cochran. It unfolded on the No. 7 hole, a 136-yard, par-3 with an elevated tee that overlooks a small pond and an island green.

Jerry Towns pulled out his 8-iron. He was playing with his uncle, Gene Towns, and Tom Fisher. Fisher, as it turns out, had an appropriate name for what happened next.

"Jerry hit his shot high, with a lot of backspin," said Gene Towns. "It landed about 6 feet on the green, but it spun back off the green into the water."

Jerry Towns has been playing golf only about two years. Hitting the green with backspin is the goal of every golfer. For a novice like Towns, just hitting the green is a reward.

"I was pretty disgusted," he said. "I quickly turned around and started heading back to the cart. Then I heard the sound a bass makes when he hits something in the water. I didn't think anything about it at first. Then my uncle said: 'Come here. You're not going to believe this.'"

The ball had trickled into a bass bed a few feet off the bank. When the Pinnacle plopped into the water, a hungry young large-mouth bass measuring about 14 inches long and weighing about one pound, thought he was getting an after-school snack.

"There was a swirl when that fish started charging the ball," said Gene Towns. "Then there was another swirl. That fish had the ball in its mouth and made a 360-degree circle back to the point where it had picked up the ball. I was looking at the ball as it came from under the water. It was like an imaginary hand just took it and threw it back on the green."

Said Fisher: "I don't think we had better tell anybody about this. Nobody is going to believe us."

Jerry Towns missed his birdie, but he settled for somewhat of a bassackwards par.

"I was shocked," he said. "If it had been in a tournament I don't know what I would have done." Nothing in the rules of golf addressed this particular situation.

"He had plenty of room to putt without even thinking about getting his feet wet," said Gene Towns. "When we got to the green, that fish was still there in the bed. His fins were up. He was angry."

Course co-owner Charlton Norris has seen some strange things happen on the seventh hole at The Woods. A woman once pulled out a driver, skipped her tee shot across the pond three times and had the ball run up on the green for a hole-in-one.

But, unless there is a UFO sighting, nothing will top the fish story.

"People laughed and were checking our carts to see if we were drinking," said Gene Towns. "But it's the truth. My name and reputation are standing on it. I'm sure it's going to be a joke around here for years to come. People already are talking about the 'trained' fish. I really don't know how to explain it. It's just a phenomenon."

Jerry Towns, 39, is a corrections officer at the Dodge Correctional Institute. After telling his wife and children about the fluke shot, he mentioned it to several co-workers. "

Some of them looked at me kind of strange," he said. "One time when I was hunting, I killed two quail with one shot. But that was bound to happen sooner or later. The odds of this happening again are a trillion to one."

When it comes to golf and fish stories, this one is a keeper.

A victory in de-feet

September 16, 1995

Chris Diehl's story has a happy ending. Call it a footnote. Consider it victory in de-feet. It is the tale of a teen-ager's frustration, a mother's desperation, a pro football team's reaction and, finally, a family's elation.

Diehl is just your average 6-foot-4, 235-pound high school freshman with a size-17 shoe.

He's always been a head — or two or three — taller than his ninth-grade classmates at Macon's Tattnall Square Academy. He even dwarfs his dad, Leon, who is 6-foot-3.

"Chris and one of his cousins were born six days apart," said his mother, Glenda Diehl. "If you stand them together, they look six years apart."

Glenda Diehl admits she had no premonition when Chris checked into the world on Nov. 22, 1980. He weighed 8 pounds at birth, nothing out of the ordinary.

"But, from that point on, he just started growing," she said. "He weighed 32 pounds when he was 1 year old. We went to the pediatrician, and he already was off the growth chart. We knew he was going to be a big child. We just didn't know he would keep growing like this."

The mother soon became accustomed to making such adjustments. Don't let anyone kid you. One size doesn't fit all. At 18 months, Chris was wearing 3T (3-year-old toddler) outfits. She remembers buying a pair of Buster Brown shoes for him to wear to Sunday school. Three weeks later, his foot had shot from a size 3 to a 5. She couldn't have gotten them on him with a crowbar.

Glenda Diehl believes her son inherited his size from her late father, Homer Glen Alt, who lived in West Virginia. If she thought she had it rough coping with her son's sizes when he was a child, the problems grew as he grew. By the time Chris became a teen-ager, his feet were growing faster than the national deficit.

"I used to think my only challenges would be that he would grow so fast and grow out of his clothes," she said.

As an eighth-grade lineman on Tattnall's junior varsity last season, Diehl wore a size-14 cleat. The selection wasn't always the best, but with frequent trips to Atlanta and frantic calls to mail-order companies, the Diehls at least could locate shoes.

The legwork really began when his foot jumped to a size 17 this season, and the family could not find footwear anywhere. In early August, with no cleat marks in sight, Glenda Diehl took back-to-school shopping to a new level. At the suggestion of a family friend, she wrote all 30 NFL teams about her son's predicament.

Within a month, she had replies from about half the pro teams. Most were polite responses. They said they couldn't help because they had no players wearing that large of a shoe. One note was from New York Giants coach Dan Reeves, who took a personal interest because Reeves is a native of nearby Americus.

The phone call that made the difference was from the Atlanta Falcons' front office. What better person to handle a foot crisis than the man who made his own feet famous — Billy "White Shoes" Johnson?

"We were happy to try to accommodate him," said Johnson, the former Falcons wide receiver who is now director of player programs. "We have several players who wear a size 15 or 16, but the only one who wore a 17 was Lincoln Kennedy. I spoke with Lincoln, and he understood the young man's plight. He had a similar problem getting shoes when he was growing up. He was kind to help. I'm sorry I couldn't. I only wear a 9 1/2."

Chris Diehl and his family were invited to the Falcons training complex in Suwanee, where they met Johnson and toured the facilities, including a visit to Kennedy's locker. Although the 6-foot-6, 325-pound offensive tackle was not there, he left Diehl with two pairs of turf training shoes, one pair of Apex cleats and another pair of Nike Air Jordan tennis shoes.

The cleats, which had been worn briefly by Kennedy, surfaced just in time for Diehl to use them in Tattnall's first B-team game against Westfield a week ago. By coincidence, Diehl was issued a No. 75 home jersey, the same number worn by Kennedy.

"Chris loves the movie 'Forrest Gump,' " said Glenda Diehl. "When he got these shoes, I told him they could be his own magic shoes."

The New York Giants later located a pair of size-17 black Reebok pump cleats and sent them a few days ago. Glenda Diehl also found a pair from a mail-order firm. After facing the possibility of starting the season with no football shoes, the Diehls have a foothold on good fortune.

"This is the most shoes I've had in my whole life," Chris said.

His parents have encouraged him to continue to play football, although Chris admits his feet can be a hindrance. He is the slowest player on the team. His mother still smiles when she reaches for a figurine of a football player, given to her by her mother, Wilma Alt, when Chris was 2 years old. It's as if playing football is his destiny.

She said the experience with his shoes has helped her son go from low self-esteem to growing confidence. After all, there aren't too many JV football players who are wearing shoes once filled by an NFL first-round draft choice.

"Now his friends probably wish they had big feet, too," she said, laughing.

Of course, her laughter can quickly be replaced by a look of terror. She winces at the thought of a still-growing foot. The largest shoe size listed in the Guinness Book of World Records is a size 23, worn by a 22-year-old Pennsylvania man named Matthew McGrory.

"We're well-taken care of now. We just hope and pray we can get through the season without his foot growing any more," said Glenda Diehl. "We went from a 14 last year to a 17 this year. I'd hate to be thinking next year we'd be looking at a 20."

If the shoe fits, find it.

Because it's the law, son!

February 7, 1997

Some would argue against its merits but a significant piece of legislation began working its way through the political process this week.

Mark Burkhalter, a state representative from Alpharetta, wants to make it a crime to toss a cigarette butt out a car window.

The state does not recognize this as littering. Burkhalter believes it should be a misdemeanor. It's nasty. It's dangerous. (No confirmed reports, though, on whether there are rival gangs running around north Atlanta engaging in this criminal activity. If there were, maybe they could call themselves the Pall Malls and the Marlboro Men.)

Flicking your Brown & Williamson out the window at the corner of Third and Plum might not seem like much of an argument for seeking the death penalty. And it certainly seems trivial when you stack it next to welfare reform, pay raises for teachers, drunken driving legislation, utility deregulation and budget cuts.

But it shouldn't be dismissed if it's something that impacts our everyday lives. I saw somebody take a long draw and then chunk their cigarette out the car window the other day. It was still smoking as they drove off. It burned me up so much I was tempted to chase them down and make a citizen's arrest.

I recently attended the 10th Annual Government Affairs Conference in Atlanta. While chewing on some fried chicken and listening to some pork barrel, I wanted to reach into my pocket and produce a list of useful laws I would love to recommend. I should have used the opportunity to suggest that our lawmakers introduce, approve and implement some meaningful, in-your-face laws — like cigarette-tossing.

By my own calculations, with a margin of error of roughly 31.3 percent, approximately 68.7 percent of the more than 2,000 pieces of legislation being considered will have little or no bearing on our lives.

Certainly our legislators could go to bat for us on other issues that really matter, such as getting rid of those annoying station logos at the bottom of the TV screen. Or the next time our children stay up past their bed time, we would have legislation on our side to help us win the battle.

"It's 9:30. Go to bed, son."

"But why, Dad?"

"Because it's the law, that's why!"

Here are others. My list keeps growing every day.

There ought to be a law that:

• It should never be allowed to rain on a Saturday.

• Fruitcake should be banished from the face of the earth.

• Anyone who doesn't use deodorant should have to pay extra taxes.

• Fine print should be banned from all advertising.

• If the Atlanta Braves don't start winning more than one out of every four World Series, they should give fans a full refund.

• Kids who don't turn in their homework during the week should be required to go to school on weekends.

• People who go through the supermarket's 14-item line with 23 items should be executed on the spot.

• Any phone call, solicited or otherwise, that interrupts supper should be subject to heavy fines.

• All professional wrestling should be exported to Alabama.

• Bumper stickers that say: "My child is an honor student at ...." should be outlawed. (Hint: Tell your kid how proud you are you, not your bumper.)

• Anyone whining for more than 30 minutes on any given day should be required to perform 100 hours of community service.

• Not only should they raise the age to get a driver's license to 18 but, right before my oldest son turns 18, they should raise it to 21.

• Fast-food hamburgers should be required to taste better than the wrapper they are served in.

• Everyone should be encouraged to carry a library card and use it.

• Anyone elected to serve on Macon City Council must be able to do more sit-ups than Mayor Jim Marshall.

Part Five

Lightning Bugs Don't
Come in a Jar

Pearl comes out of her shell

April 1978

"...Boy, I hadn't had a skate key in my hands in years. It didn't feel funny though. You could put a skate key in my hands fifty years from now, in pitch dark, and I'd still know what it is."

— *The Catcher in the Rye.*

Some of the most precious pieces of our lives often can be found deep inside some forgotten drawer or pocket. They are remnants and souvenirs of bygone days that have been put aside by the march of time yet still guarded by our memories.

Some objects are of little value, but we cannot bear to throw them away. Like the skate key Holden Caufield finds in J. D. Salinger's "The Catcher in the Rye," excitement, power and emotion can be generated in an act of rediscovery.

And so it was with Pearl. I opened the drawer, and there she was. She did not look past me, but right at me. It was the reunion of two long, lost friends.

Her face was long and angelic. She had a narrow nose with no nostrils. She had inkmarks on her chin and holes in her head from where her hair had lovingly been pulled out. Her tiny dress was blue with patterned butterflies. Some people called them bugs. But, to me, they were always butterflies.

She had little or no mouth with which to smile, but then she didn't have to smile. Her eyes did that for her. She had no tongue with which to speak, but all she had to do was listen.

It was Pearl, my doll.

I had tucked her away in some obscure drawer years ago and had forgotten about her. I had slid rows of folded clothes past her and never cared to notice.

While I was busy becoming educated, sophisticated and manipulated, she had been patiently awaiting my return.

And now, suddenly, I was here again. It was like I never left. Holden Caufield had found the key to unlock his past, and now I had found mine.

Pearl was from an era when things were different. Backyard worlds were larger. Responsibilities were fewer. Trouble was something we managed daily, and love was the only four-letter word we knew.

There were cartwheels instead of car wheels, crayons in place of typewriters. On Saturday mornings, we watched "Bullwinkle" and "Mighty Mouse" instead of "The Robonic Stooges" and "Space Academy." We ate Hershey bars and Chiclets instead of Ding-A-Lings and Space Dust.

Life was a lot less complicated.

Pearl was pitiful. I don't know why my mother ever bought her. Pearl was a Phyllis Diller reject. She looked like she just stepped out of a horror flick. She was uglier than the south end of a horse traveling north.

My sister had rejected her. Pretty baby girls should have pretty baby dolls. So, Pearl was mine. Not by reward, but by forfeit.

Oh, I pulled off her arms and legs occasionally. They always went back on. I pulled her hair out, too. It never went back on. I did leave a curly lock on her forehead. That was for me to stroke every night while I went to sleep.

I remember a time in Nashville when Mom made Dad turn the car around so we could retrieve a lost Pearl from underneath a motel room bed. The motel maid was about to put her away, but somehow Pearl had survived.

And, through the years, so had I. I had put Pearl away, but only for a while. Now I was entering the world of rediscovery.

I looked at her. Pearl was ugly. But that is what made her so beautiful.

I lifted her from the cluttered drawer and stroked that magical strand of hair that had survived. She had no mouth with which to speak. But all she had to do was listen.

There are some things I hope I never outgrow.

Dressed like a dog

Sept. 28, 1985

ATHENS—The dog is sprawled in the doorway, his skin drooping off his upper body and onto the floor like an oversized coat.

Outside, a cool breeze is prematurely hinting the arrival of football weather, and a campus splashed in red and black is anticipating the hour before kickoff.

Inside, it is warm, and the white English bulldog is feeling the effects of a hearty breakfast. He is sleepy, and pays little attention to the commotion that is building around him.

Frank "Sonny" Seiler, the dog's owner, is sitting on a nearby bed in an upstairs room at the University of Georgia's Center for Continuing Education. He looks at his watch and then claps his hands loudly.

"Mmweeewanammmphugwee (or something phonetically close to this)," Seiler bellows in a high-pitched voice.

This is not a language human beings can understand. But Uga IV, the mascot for the University of Georgia, hears the command and springs into action. Anticipating the event that is about to happen, he charges toward Seiler like a blitzing linebacker.

It is time for the dressing of the dog.

An audience has gathered for the traditional ceremony, but Uga doesn't seem to mind getting dressed in front of a crowd. This is not a silly sideshow. To Seiler, the ritual must be performed exactly right.

"I'm very superstitious," says Seiler, pulling an outfit from Uga's personal tote bag.

Uga puts on his game jersey just like any other dog—one leg at a time. But Seiler, a Savannah attorney who has furnished Ugas I, II and III as Georgia mascots from the same bloodline since 1956, is very particular about selecting the right attire.

"Daddy's very funny about which jersey Uga wears," said Seiler's daughter, Swann. "He's more superstitious about some jerseys. If Uga has had good luck with a jersey, he'll wear that.

"Daddy keeps up with all the jerseys. If it's hot, Uga wears a lightweight outfit. He has quite a wardrobe. The mood and climate of Athens determines what he wears."

On this particular day, Uga is sporting a new jersey. The one he wore in an opening loss to Alabama has joined other losing outfits "somewhere," as Seiler puts it, "in the outer limits of hell."

For years, Uga's red outfits were stitched by Seiler's wife, Cecelia. Now, they are made from the same durable material as the players' jerseys and tailor-made by Nonnie Sutton, a professional seamstress from Norcross.

Uga might go through as many as a half-dozen outfits in one season. He has torn them while frolicking among the hedges at Sanford Stadium. And still others have been called to the graveyard after a Georgia loss.

Before Seiler pulls the red jersey over Uga's wrinkled brow, the dog is doused with baby powder to whiten the splotches in his white hair and to make him smell nice. Of course, he's already had his traditional bath and pedicure—or pet-i-cure, if you will—the night before.

After the jersey is fitted over Uga's short legs and the black letter "G" squarely centered on his broad chest, Seiler puts the famous spike collar around his pet's neck.

It's time to go, an anxious Uga seems to say, and turns toward the door. Go Dogs!

Following the cue, the Seiler family and dozens of Georgia fans tag along. The elevator doors open, and Uga eagerly hops on.

Elevators are one of his passions in life, along with riding in wheelbarrows, signing autographs (with shoe polish on his paw) and eating Varsity hot dogs (hold the mustard).

Downstairs, Uga strolls through the lobby as if he owns the place. Years ago, when the Continuing Education building first opened, pets were not allowed in the motel rooms, and Uga's forefathers had to be snuck up and down the fire escape at the end of the hall.

Now, after having stayed at the Ritz Carlton, the Hilton and other fine hotels all over the country, Uga IV could order room service if he wanted. Said Swann: "He's traveled better than most people."

This trip will be a short one, though, down Lumpkin Street and into the parking lot under the bridge at Sanford Stadium. There, he sits on the Seiler's red station wagon like a king on his throne. Fans have been stopping by for years to pat his head for good luck before the game.

"He tolerates crowds extremely well," said Swann Seiler. "Just think, if your head was patted for a couple of hours each Saturday, you probably wouldn't like it."

After Georgia's Redcoat Band marches onto the field, it is time for Uga to make his ceremonial entrance with the cheerleaders and players. Since 1956, the four Ugas have been seen by more than 15 million spectators and millions more on television.

So, as you can see, it's important for Uga to look his best. No matter how the Dogs look on the field, this dog at least can rest assured he's dressed for the part.

Claus encounters of the bearded kind

Dec.17, 1996

Yes, Virginia, Derek, Tony, Brandon and Ruth. There is a Santa Claus.

I know because I had coffee with him at the Galleria Mall in Centerville. He took me into a back office and let me sit in his recliner. That was quite an honor. We ate chocolate chip cookies, laughed at his stories and he told me: "I couldn't imagine my life without this."

Yes, there is a Santa. I know because I could see the twinkle behind his Ben Franklin, wire-rimmed glasses. And Mrs. Claus was there, too, going through the boxes of mail on the table. One letter was from a little girl who listed no less than 17 toys she wanted to be deposited under the tree. At least she had the courtesy to add a P.S. at the bottom: "You really don't have to bring me *all* of these things, Santa."

It was windy the afternoon I dropped by to see Santa Claus, and he apologized for the way it had rushed through his beard like a twister. Of course, the children always end up pulling at his hair anyway to check its authenticity. They also tug away at the buttons and seams of his clothes, which is why Santa keeps a dozen safety pins fastened to the inside of his vest. "The pins are for blowouts," he explained.

He told me about the young boy who made a recent trip from a town more than 100 miles away. The child had refused to believe in him, so Santa did his homework. He researched the boy's home, favorite food and even his teacher's name. When the boy climbed up onto his lap, Santa was ready.

"I told him all these things only Santa would know, and his eyes got real big," said Santa. "But when his dad asked him about it later, the little boy said: 'Well, he's a nice old man, but the poor thing really does think he's Santa.'"

He is. Honest. Just ask Brenda Murphy, who showed up with her 8-year-old son, Alex Fletcher, on a recent afternoon. She watched the jolly old man convince her son that, if there was no Santa, then who would feed the reindeer? "I'm not so sure myself that he isn't actually Santa Claus," she said.

"I have some children who are 13 or 14 years old, and they still believe," said Santa. "And I have some that are 5 years old who don't want to believe. If I can just get a non-believer on my lap, I can get him believing again. I always tell them this: 'If you don't believe, you won't receive.'"

His most unusual request ever was for five pounds of pecans. He told me about the young boy who wanted a bicycle last year and asked for a bike again this year. Seems as if he parked it in his back yard one afternoon and, when he came back, the bike was gone. A dog was laying on the same spot where he left the bike. "He honestly believed that dog ate it," laughed Santa.

Between sips of coffee and nibbles on his cookie, Santa told me about the blind boy who comes to see him every year. The boy touches the buckles on the man's boots and hair on his chin to make sure he's got the right Santa. Once, Santa gave him a bell off his sleigh. Another time, he gave him the bullwhip he uses to jumpstart the reindeer.

"The other day, I had a little girl ask me if I could bring her mother home from Korea for Christmas," Santa said. "She walked away, and then came back and said: 'If you can't bring her home, could you ask her to send us $300 for a trampoline?' "

Mrs. Claus nodded at the stories and smiled. "One day," she said, "we are going to have to write a book."

Santa sees something special reflected in the eyes of the children, and each generation renews the spirit. Moms and dads sometimes have to wipe away their own tears when they realize they once sat in the very same chair. Another Santa used it at Westgate Mall in Macon more than 31 years ago.

Sometimes the children will ride on his new train. Other times he reads them "The Night Before Christmas" or sings them a Christmas song he wrote to the tune of "She'll Be Coming 'Round the Mountain."

Often, he tells them he knows about the fight they had with their brother or sister in the car on the way over to the mall. Santa knows *everything*. The younger ones sometimes bring him their pacifiers, bottles and blankets as a testament to growing up. But Mrs. Claus is wise. She always keeps them handy, just in case they need to come back.

And some of them do come back, the same way Santa always comes back. It's comforting, just like the words to my favorite Christmas song. It's the Roger Miller tune, "Old Toy Trains," where a child anxiously waits for Santa's arrival on Christmas Eve. *"Close your eyes. Listen to the skies. ..."*

"We would like to keep doing this forever," Mrs. Claus said, softly.

Yes, Virginia, Reggie, Andrew, Candace and Tomeka.

No matter how old you get, that's always reassuring to know.

Part Six

All I Need to Know,
I Learned in a Press Box

100 reasons why I love football

August 25, 1997

I can think of at least 37 reasons why I like country music and 14 reasons why I'm afraid of snakes.

I've always been able to come up with at least 21 reasons why I couldn't eat all my vegetables as a kid.

Now I can think of 43 reasons why you never should discuss politics at the dinner table.

I can easily mark down 68 reasons why I would rather play golf than cut the grass on Saturday mornings. I can offer 29 reasons why I'd rather read a book than see the movie.

But football? I can think of more reasons why I love football than just about anything.

There are as many reasons to explain my passion as there are stripes on a football field. So, in honor of the start of another season, I bring to you the 100 reasons why I love football.

1. Emmitt Smith. 2. Tailgating. 3. The four seasons: Regular season, bowl season, recruiting season and spring practice. 4. The four Joes: Paterno, Namath, Gibbs and Montana. 5. The Northside–Warner Robins rivalry.

6. John Heisman: "The true football fan pays no attention to time or mileage when there is a big game to see." 7. Buck Belue to Lindsay Scott. 8. Pat Sullivan to Terry Beasley. 9. Joe Montana to Jerry Rice. 10. Georgia-Georgia Tech jokes: Did you hear about the Georgia player who was dropped from the team for breaking training? The coach caught him studying.

11. Flea-flickers, fumblerooskis, the Statue of Liberty and the oldest trick in the playbook—the tackle eligible. 12. Super Bowl parties. 13. Passing through a small town on a Friday night and seeing those stadium lights fill a pocket in the night sky. 14. Gutsy coaches who go for it on fourth-and-goal. 15. Goal-line stands.

16. It's one of the few sports where there still is a pregame prayer. 17. The definition of an atheist in Alabama: Someone who doesn't believe in Bear Bryant. 18. A University of Georgia bumper sticker

from the early 1980s: "God Bless You, Mrs. Walker." 19. Hail Mary. 20. Touchdown Jesus.

21. The beauty of watching Danny Wuerffel throw the football. 22. The satisfaction of watching Steve Spurrier throw his visor. 23. An excuse to delay all those New Year's resolutions about not eating junk food until after the bowl games. 24. Resorting to couch potato status on an NFL Sunday afternoon. 25. Having the game get so exciting that you wind up jumping up and down on the couch.

26. That I'm old enough to remember watching Archie Manning play and young enough to appreciate Peyton Manning. 27. The Terrible Towel. 28. The Crying Towel. 29. Gatorade baths for coaches, now available in different flavors. 30. A game where everyone is a designated hitter.

31. Between the Hedges at Sanford Stadium. 32. Strolls down North Avenue at Georgia Tech. 33. Howard's Rock at Clemson. 34. Saturday night in Baton Rouge. 35. Beautiful Eagle Creek.

36. The fact that there's always a week to prepare for the next game and a week to get over the last one. 37. The comfort of knowing there still are a few coaches out there who know how to run the "Notre Dame box." 38. Forging a friendship with someone simply because you share the same favorite play from a game 12 years ago. 39. The only place where pompoms and shakers are entirely appropriate. 40. Leonard's Losers.

41. Two Terrys—Bowden and Bradshaw. 42. Two Bobbys—Dodd and Ross. 43. Two Barrys—Switzer and Sanders. 44. Two Vinces—Lombardi and Dooley. 45. Two Steves—Young and Bartkowski.

46. Just out of curiosity, checking the point spread at the start of every week. 47. Always remembering that Goliath once was a heavy favorite over David. 48. Bobby Bowden's own suggested epitaph: "...But He Played Miami." 49. Shug Jordan's Seven D's for success: Discipline, Desire to Excel, Dedication, Determination, Dependability, Desperation and, Damn It Anyway. 50. Pep rallies and bonfires.

51. Walk-ons. 52. Armchair quarterbacks. 53. A South Georgia high school coach once telling me that if you didn't win in his league, someone would drop a suitcase on your doorstep and put a "For Sale" sign in your front yard. 54. Frank Howard's reason for stepping down at Clemson: "I retired for health reasons. The alumni were sick of me." 55. Bum Phillips' similar lament: "Every coach is an interim coach."

56. Halftime shows: The only breaks that are truly worth it in sports (except for the seventh-inning stretch). 57. Watching the Dallas Cowboys between bites of turkey on Thanksgiving. 58. The Citrus Bowl, clearly the most entertaining bowl trip if you're a player (or a sports writer). 59. The Southeastern Conference Championship Game in

Atlanta, the next-best thing to a bowl game. 60. A downfield block that I once threw in the final game of my high school career that led to a touchdown. And having my old high school coach still bring it up whenever we talk on the phone. (Like that Pizza Hut commercial, it gets even better with time.)

61. Doug Porter, one more year for a class act. 62. George O'Leary, one of the wittiest in the business. 63. Dan Pitts, the legend still going strong at Mary Persons. 64. Billy Henderson, thanks for the memories. 65. Gene Stallings, the only coach I know who can recite Rudyard Kipling by heart.

66. The Grits Blitz. 67. Recruiting nuts who know every height, weight, SAT score and time in the 40-yard-dash. 68. November playoff games where you can see your breath, can't feel your hands and the lines are long for hot chocolate. 69. Hearing people at the grocery store, barber shop and gas station all talking about the big game on Friday night. 70. Auburn-Alabama jokes: How do you tell an Auburn funeral procession? The tractors all have their lights on.

71. Monday Night Football. Even without Howard Cosell, it sure beats watching Murphy Brown. 72. Erk Russell's philosophy: "If you don't have the best of everything, make the best of everything you have." 73. The Macon Midget Football League. 74. Chris Hatcher and all the other under-sized overachievers. 75. Positions with names like bandit and scatback. You won't find that in soccer.

76. Two-point conversions. 77. Three-point stances. 78. The Fearsome Foursome. 79. Nickel defenses. 80. Six-point underdogs.

81. Sandlot games as a kid. Never touch, always tackle. 82. Having my Dad once take me to see Gale Sayers play. 83. Getting choked up whenever I watch "Brian's Song." 84. Once trying to figure out which one I liked better: Johnny Unitas, Bart Starr or Don Meredith. 85. Now trying to figure out which one I like better: Jim Harbaugh, Brett Favre or Troy Aikman.

86. The Macon Touchdown Club. 87. The sounds of a marching band warming up in the parking lot before the game. 88. Pride that junior college football is alive and well at Middle Georgia and Georgia Military College. 89. Watching a game evolve from players going "both ways" to one so specialized it has snappers, holders and sometimes even "pooch" punters. 90. The fun of trying to out-pick the "experts" every week.

91. Valdosta. The best high school football town in America. 92. Listening to coaches downplay their own team while exalting the strengths of their opponent. 93. Jack Kemp: "Pro football gave me a good sense of perspective to enter politics. I already had been booed, cheered, cut, sold, traded and hung in effigy." 94. All the debates about

who is No. 1 in college football. 95. Sitting around with some high school coaches and studying their faces as they study film.

96. Keeping in mind that the first two Super Bowls were just as lopsided as the last five. 97. South Carolina-Clemson jokes: What do you get a Clemson bride who has registered her wedding gifts? Her favorite brand of socket wrench. 98. The movie, "Rudy." 99. Andy Griffith's old recording, "What It Was, Was Football." 100. Because, as someone once said, the ball always takes funny bounces.

Ed Grisamore

Bubbas, bombs, bricks, bronze, blimps...

August 5, 1996

ATLANTA—What we choose to remember about the Olympics is largely up to us.

It could be Billy, Bubba, bombs, bricks, bronze, basketball, blimps, buses, barricades, badminton or this Bud's for you.

Right now, I can remember almost everything I've done for the past 19 days. I can remember where I was sitting during the Opening Ceremonies, where I was standing when I saw Michael Johnson sprint into history. I even can remember what I ate for supper the night I went to watch team handball.

It's all still fresh. It's all still rattling around in my head. Some of it's clogged. Only time will clear-cut it.

But it's not what I remember now that's important. It's the staying power of what I will remember 20 years from now. It's what I will tell the grandchildren when they gather around the television to watch Kerri Strug sprain her ankle trying to light the Olympic flame in the Summer Games in Topeka in the year 2024.

These are the memories that I will take with me:

• Angel Martino, of Americus, winning a bronze in swimming on the first day of competition, then giving the medal to a friend with cancer.

"She's my hero," Martino said. "She helps me remember the things that are important in life."

What a great way to start the Olympics. What a great way to remember them.

• Having a security guard tell me the metal detectors at the venues were so sensitive they could pick up the aluminum foil on a chewing gum wrapper. Then, having a friend tell me he had gone through with his keys in his pocket all week and the alarm had sounded only one time.

• The Pocket Hercules. I never had seen an international weightlifting competition until I saw Turkey's 4-foot-11 Naim

Suleymanoglu win a record third Olympic gold and lift the spirit of a nation with him.

What made it special was sitting by five Turkish journalists, who stood and cheered and strained with him on every snatch. If this had happened in the press box at an American football or baseball game they would have been booted out. Cheering at the press table is considered a capital offense in journalism ethics.

I looked over at them when he had pocketed his medal. They were crying.

• The bomb. Why must we always remember the bad? Because I was shaking for 20 minutes after I heard about the blast at Centennial Park. Because someone in our Knight-Ridder bureau at the Main Press Center put a photograph of Alice Hawthorne on the bulletin board with a note: "Remember the Victim." Because we are inclined to worry so much about international terrorism that we tend to overlook that we also have to be protected from ourselves.

• A Czechoslovakian named Jan Zelezny, who became the first javelin thrower in 72 years to repeat as gold medalist. He says he wants to be a pitcher for the Atlanta Braves. Anyone for a starting rotation of Smoltz, Maddux, Glavine and Zelezny?

• Muhammad Ali lighting the torch at the Opening Ceremonies. It was a great choice, followed by a touching gesture to replace the gold medal he had lost in 1960.

• The sacrilegious side of the Olympics. The hedges missing from Sanford Stadium. Aluminum bats inside Atlanta-Fulton County Stadium. The parade of nations being overshadowed by a parade of tacky street vendors in downtown Atlanta. And that thousands of foreigners will return to their home countries actually thinking that "YMCA" is our national anthem.

• Catching a bus downtown and realizing that the bus driver and I were the only ones who spoke English.

• Most will remember the courage of Kerri Strug, who vaulted into America's hearts on a sprained ankle. Soon, you'll see her face on a box of Wheaties.

I will choose to remember Gillian Rolton, a 40-year-old equestrian competitor from Australia. She tumbled off her horse and broke her collarbone and two ribs but got up and led her country to the gold medal.

• I will remember Dot Richardson's enthusiasm, Kurt Angle's tears, Amy Van Dyken's smile, Dan O'Brien's redemption and Kim Batten's disappointment.

• And I will remember Izzy, may he R.I.P. By late Sunday, this was the scuttlebutt: Now that the Olympics are over, will Izzy become a Wuzzy?

To be great is to be misunderstood

February 20, 1996

The words now haunt. Maybe they didn't mean much at the time. Maybe they were said in a different context, not meant to be prophetic.

But, on an August day five years ago, Wayne McDuffie propped his feet up on his office desk and talked about accepting the challenge of becoming Georgia's offensive coordinator.

"I knew it was going to be a difficult job," he said. "My wife thinks it might kill me. Well, you've got to die sometime."

They buried Wayne McDuffie on Monday, three days after he apparently aimed a gun at his heart and pulled the trigger. Family and friends, from Tallahassee to Athens to his hometown in Hawkinsville, sorted through their own heartaches and tried to understand.

Will anyone ever understand? Ralph Waldo Emerson once said: "To be great is to be misunderstood."

Many knew of Wayne McDuffie, but few *knew* him. He always could find time for you, but never would reveal much of himself. He threw up the guard, and he often was viewed as distant and aloof. He was driven to win everything but popularity contests.

In December, he went down with Ray Goff's sinking ship. Over the past two months, he had drawn blanks on job offers after trips to the Senior Bowl and NFL scouting combine. On Friday, two days after Valentine's Day and the same day Goff received a troubling letter from him, McDuffie became a statistic. Every day in the U.S., an estimated 89 people commit suicide.

He was as respected as any assistant football coach in Georgia history, and he was one of the most brilliant offensive minds in college football. The Bulldogs failed to win a Southeastern Conference championship not because of McDuffie's offenses but because their defenses never measured up.

His desk always was stacked with game film, scouting reports and boxes of Tylenol. There was a sheet and blanket on the sofa in his office, and he often slept there.

Behind the scenes, he was legendary. In 1977, on his first tour of duty at Georgia, he stood up in front of the other assistants on Vince Dooley's staff and told them they were aiming too low by simply recruiting to win the SEC title. "Dammit," he said, "you can compete for the national championship at Georgia. ... The state is full of football players. You get the best athletes in the state of Georgia, and you can compete with anybody."

That same year, he recruited and delivered Valdosta quarterback Buck Belue to play in Athens. Three years later, Georgia won the national championship.

When he was offensive coordinator at Florida State in 1988, he slammed his fist on a table at a coaches meeting and told the staff they would be crazy not to sign quarterback Charlie Ward up the road in Thomasville. Ward won the Heisman Trophy. The Seminoles won the national championship.

But, while a visionary, he also was a loner. Despite being progressive in his thinking, he was a throwback to the old school.

I once told someone McDuffie was born 20 years too late. If Bear Bryant, Woody Hayes and Vince Lombardi still were roaming the sidelines, McDuffie would have fit right in among them.

"I used to think he was the biggest S.O.B. this side of the Mississippi," said Macon native Jeff Harper, who played for McDuffie at Georgia in 1980. "But if you had it in you, he'd get it out of you."

He was gruff and in-your-face, not the articulate, media-friendly, alumni-loving glamour boy. Football under McDuffie was life in the Marines. He always was looking, as he put it, for "a few good men, not a bunch of people wasting my time." He rarely was mentioned for head coaching jobs. He seemed destined to be a career assistant coach.

His mother, Elise McDuffie, still lives in Hawkinsville. So does his high school coach, Bobby Gentry. The caption below McDuffie's senior picture in the 1963 Hawkinsville High School yearbook reads: "Some think he's bashful, but others know better."

Then again, had we known him even better we might understand why this man inflicted a violent mark upon himself. Was it disappointment, depression or anger?

In death, as in life, Wayne McDuffie played hard.

Chip off the old ice block

January 22, 1994

What were the odds? Probably a billion to one.

What were his chances? A snowball rolling down Cherry Street in July had a better one.

Chip Minton has earned a seat on the U.S. Olympic bobsled team. That's Chip Minton of Macon, Ga., not Chip Minton of Aspen, Colo., or Schenectady, N.Y.

Write a movie script. Sell it to Hollywood. Call it Cool Runnings.

Sure, Macon has produced its share of renowned sports heroes over the years, but never an Olympic bobsledder.

And even though Jack Frost sometimes throws a blanket on Coleman Hill on January mornings, Macon isn't exactly a winter sports mecca. We produce basketball players, not Nordic skiers. We develop gymnasts, not figure skaters.

That's why, from the beginning, Minton appeared to be longer than a longshot. The extent of his downhill racing was limited to grabbing trash can lids as a youngster and skidding through his Bloomfield neighborhood. The closest he had ever come to a bobsled was a friend name Bob, who owned a sled.

When I first met Minton 18 months ago, I wanted him to do well. He was clean-cut, polite and friendly, not some conceited jock. I liked him. I was pulling for him.

But I also expected him to eventually disappear off the screen. It happens all the time. Big dreams get squashed on baseball fields, and in tiny gyms.

The world is full of athletes with plenty of heart and not enough ability. Or plenty of talent and not enough heart.

Minton sewed the two together. He was lucky and, as it turned out, good enough to be regarded as one of the top 12 bobsledders in the nation. No, this wasn't just a joy ride.

He had stumbled into the sport almost by accident. When the U. S. Bobsled Federation held a tryout at the Tattnall Square Academy track in May 1992, Minton performed well on a six-item physical test.

His wife, Dannah, sat in the bleachers that day, pregnant with the couple's first child, and shook her head in cool amazement. "Chip is *always* trying something," she said. "But I sat there and watched and couldn't believe he was doing something like that. To be honest with you, I thought it would just fizzle out. It would be over, and he'd go do something else."

But it never stopped. It never even slowed down. About the time I suspected I had heard the last of Minton's bobsled adventure, I'd get the good word from Lake Placid, N.Y., Cortona, Italy or Calgary, Alberta. It was unbelievable. There he was, inching his way toward Lillehammer, Norway, the site of the Winter Olympics.

He would train at some of the best facilities in the world. At home, he would try to push his truck up a hill. He borrowed a 16-pound bowling ball from Gold Cup and tossed it as if it were a giant shot put, working his arm and chest muscles. His friends approached him with puzzled looks. "Bobsled? How did you ever ... ?"

There were sacrifices. Family. Job. "We saved every dime we could get our hands on," Dannah Minton said. "We moved out of our house and in with a friend just so we could pay the bills."

Minton took a leave of absence from his job as a corrections officer. Dannah, an art teacher and softball coach at Southwest, was the lone bread-winner for six months. Minton had to call long distance from Canada or Germany just to hear his young daughter, Taylor, speak her first words.

Then came the U. S. Olympic Trials in Calgary. Minton and his partner, Jim Herberich, finished strong in the two-man races and the team held its position until after the four-man events.

"There were so many times when he was close to making it, and I would mention it," Dannah Minton said. "But he would always say: 'Not yet, I've still got a long way to go.' All you want to say now is: 'Thank you, God.' At the same time, you can't believe it."

What were those odds? A billion to one?

Chip Minton never even blinked.

Godmother to the Braves

May 12, 1985

ATLANTA—It is two hours before the first pitch at Atlanta-Fulton County Stadium, but Pearl Sandow has already been in her seat for more than an hour.

Outside, several hundred people are waiting for the stadium's gates to open. But, as is the custom here, Sandow is allowed in the park early.

"I love to watch batting practice," she said, trying not to squint in the afternoon sun. "It's better than the games sometimes. I like to watch the players hit, and I wonder why they don't hit that way during the games. Of course, I know it's different pitching."

Aisle 105, Row 9, Seat 1.

The ticket belongs, always has belonged, and perhaps always will belong to a gracious, Southern lady with snow-white hair piled high on her head and an Atlanta Braves' wristwatch on her left arm.

This is Pearl's domain. She even gets mail here. She selected and purchased rights to this particular seat before the stadium opened in 1965. And she has sat in it every time the Braves have played for the past 20 years. That's 1,512 games. And counting.

"The last game I missed in Atlanta was in April 1961, when the Crackers were here," she said. "I had to miss the game because my mother had a stroke. I've been real fortunate. I haven't been sick or anything, I don't have a family, and I don't work."

It has been said that the only two certainties in life are death and taxes. Whoever made that statement must not have known Pearl Sandow was a baseball fan.

* * * * * * *

Today is Mother's Day, a day not usually reserved for a woman who never married or had children of her own. But Sandow figures she has 25 sons. And they all wear Braves uniforms.

"Oh, listen, if I were to need help, I'd yell for the Braves," she said. "I'm here every day, and they are a part of my family. It hurts me when I see something happen to them. I take up for them. All these

98

things you hear about players—I don't believe it until they tell me themselves."

Like a caring mother, Sandow has watched her Braves grow up through infancy, adolescence, some awkward teen-age years and mature into a competitive outfit called "America's Team."

Some 268 different players have worn an Atlanta uniform during the team's 20 years here. And most of those players have found a special place in their hearts for the Braves' No. 1 fan.

"Anybody who plays here for any amount of time gets to know Pearl in a special way," said Atlanta catcher Bruce Benedict. "I know every time I go out on the field, and she's sitting up there, I wave to her. She's always there—win or lose. She is a great supporter and certainly a special fan for all the players. Her dedication, through thick and thin, is what sticks out more than anything else."

Although Sandow said she does not have a "favorite son," that distinction once was held by Jerry Royster, who played for the Braves for eight years before being signed as a free agent by San Diego.

"Royster came here a little boy, and he got kicked around the first few years. I think that's why I started looking after him," she said. "I was sitting here one night and this very attractive couple came up to me. The woman asked me, 'Are you Pearl?' I said, 'Yes.' And she said, 'Well, I'm Jerry Royster's mother, and I hear you've adopted him as your grandson. I came over to tell you to take the rest of my children, too!' "

Sandow is now retired after working for 33 years in the U.S. Housing Assistance Bureau in Atlanta. "I decided it was time for me to sit back and do nothing," she said.

Nothing but watch baseball, that is.

When the Braves are on the road, she never misses a broadcast or telecast, even when the team plays late-night games on the West Coast. "Now that I'm retired, I can sleep late," she said. Her age? Well, if you think Gaylord Perry's spitball is a mystery, just ask Sandow how many candles she will blow out when she celebrates her birthday on Thursday.

"Let's just say I'm 39 and holding interest," she said, laughing. "You're just as young as you feel, anyway. The funny part is, I'm not as old as a lot of people say I am. I've been coming to these games a long time, but I started at a real early age. I couldn't move around if I were as old as some of them say I am."

Her love for baseball dates back to 1934, when she began attending Atlanta Crackers' games at Ponce de Leon Park. Ponce de Leon, like the Southern League's Crackers, is now only a memory. A parking lot covers the old ballpark, and a magnolia tree stands in what used to be center field.

But Sandow still has her old seat, which was also on Row 9 on the first-base side. It was given to her by a man when the park was being torn down and now occupies her home. "It's a great conversation piece," she said. So are the some 63 autographed balls and ticket stubs from the 19 World Series she has attended.

When the Braves are in town, her game-day routine rarely varies. She catches a bus or cab from her midtown apartment and has her pre-game meal at a nearby motel before walking to the stadium to watch batting practice.

"I don't live that far away," she said. "I couldn't live far out because I'd be afraid I couldn't get to the ballpark."

The Braves issued Sandow a lifetime pass in 1975, and she later purchased the adjoining seat. She occasionally has someone sit by her, but most of the time, it is her "junk" seat, where she keeps her purse, raincoat, radio and even a small, battery-powered television with a 2-inch screen.

After more than 1,500 games in the same seat, the odds would seem pretty good that she has caught more than her share of foul balls. Has she?

"Heck, no. I cover up and duck when I see one coming," she said. "They come by here all the time, but I'm not going to try and catch a foul ball. Marty Perez (a former infielder for the Braves) once hit one that hit me in the side and knocked the breath out of me. I thought I was dying. The lady behind me kept hitting me on the back so I could catch my breath."

Sandow is popular with the fans, who often recognize her and stop in the aisle to talk baseball. But she doesn't see herself as a celebrity. "It's just that I've been around so long," she said.

As a fan, Sandow doesn't consider herself too vocal. "I don't show my emotions that much," she said. "Of course, I suffer when they lose. But I figure they're doing the best they can."

She can't stand the "Wave," yet she can remember when there were hardly enough people in Atlanta's stadium to start a ripple.

"I've been when there were only 737 people here," she said, recalling the smallest crowd in Braves' history on Sept. 8, 1975. "We could count each other."

But that's the way it has been. Through good years and lean ones, through hot July afternoons and cool September evenings, Pearl Sandow has remained a constant godmother for Atlanta's Braves.

"I always look down for that white hair," veteran announcer Ernie Johnson said from his radio booth. "And I know she's always going to be there. She never gives up either. She always believes the Braves are going to win. She has great loyalty."

"Every year, I think this is the year we're finally going to win the pennant," said Sandow. "I tell them to hurry up. I can't hang around here forever to win a World Series."

But should her time expire before the Braves finally reach that elusive goal, Sandow has made a request before departing to that great baseball diamond in the sky.

"If I die on a game day," she said, "my undertaker already has promised me he won't bury me until after the game is over."

The Pistol is gone

January 9, 1988

Until the other day, I had not thought of Elaine in years. When the news blindsided me, as it did everyone, the memories returned. A lump in my throat. Maybe even a tear or two.

The Pistol dead at 40.

Somewhere out there, I knew Elaine was crying, too.

It had only been last Saturday, while covering the Peach Bowl, that I had been talking about Pete Maravich in the present tense. A sportswriter friend was discussing his plans for the Southeastern Conference basketball tournament in Baton Rouge in March. "You'll get to see The House That Pete Built," I told him.

I thought of the Pistol again the following day when I saw him on TV. He was in a commercial to peddle his basketball video.

Then, after his heart gave out on Tuesday, I thought of him again. And I thought of Elaine.

I had one of those schoolboy crushes on her in high school, but she only paid attention to me for one reason. We shared a common bond — our love of Pete Maravich.

I knew Elaine could never be my girl. Not only was she three years older, she was madly in love with Pistol Pete. She had his pictures plastered all over her bedroom walls.

The Omni had not been built during Maravich's early years as a pro in Atlanta, and the Hawks played their home games in Georgia Tech's Alexander Memorial Coliseum. Elaine, who was old enough to drive, would let me tag along to some of the games.

I eventually gave up on trying to win her attention and fell hopelessly in love with basketball.

We would always get to the games early to watch warm-ups. Elaine's purpose for being there was to catch the Pistol's eye. For me, it was worth the price of admission just to watch Maravich shoot layups before the game.

The summer before I lost touch with Elaine, she had devised a clever plan to meet him. He lived in an apartment complex about five miles from the Atlanta suburb where we lived. She had this wild idea about driving over there and sideswiping Maravich's car in the parking lot. Of course he wouldn't be mad, she reasoned, once she'd swept him off his feet. They'd get married. Soon, she'd have a bunch of baby Pistols running around the house.

Elaine wanted me to serve as an accomplice in this elaborate and premeditated scheme. I would have no part of it. She went over there anyway, but was too much of a coward to carry out her mission.

I eventually forgot about Elaine, but Pete Maravich was—and always will be—my favorite basketball player. If imitation is the sincerest form of flattery, Maravich should have been flattered. I don't know any basketball-loving kid of my generation who did not try to pattern himself after the Pistol.

From his shaggy hair to his floppy socks, he was the very essence of basketball flamboyance. Gosh, what a talent. He was a wizard with a magic wand, waving it with an array of amazing shots and deft ball-handling.

He was a showboat, yes, but a grand and glorious one. Sometimes, he was even perceived as a brat. My mother felt that way about him, based on the one time she saw him play.

My father had promised to take me to a Hawks' game for my 16th birthday, but he had to work. So my mom took me. That night, the cool and cocky Maravich wasn't exactly a model of good sportsmanship. "He was misbehaving so badly I wanted to go right down there and shake him," my mother said. "Here all these young boys were idolizing him, and he was carrying on like that." (My mom never approved of my Raquel Welch poster, either. Moms are just that way.)

I could have cared less about the way he acted. I marveled at the way he played the game. Eventually, as we all know, Maravich settled down and became a fine Christian and dedicated family man. As it turned out, he wasn't such a bad role model after all.

Only no one ever dreamed we'd be searching for words to eulogize his passing at 40. At 80, maybe, but not at 40.

Sports heroes come and go out of our lives like the changing of the seasons. We admire them for a while, then quickly discard them to make room for a new set.

None, however, have such a lasting effect on us as those we admire when we're young. We never forget those childhood heroes. They are enduring.

Pete Maravich was not just another basketball player. He was my basketball player.

I'll miss him. But I feel richer for having seen the Pistol fire away.

I know Elaine, wherever she is, feels that way, too.

Doctors save lives,
coaches save souls

November 10, 1996

COLUMBUS—He knew he would cry. He knew that, when it was over, the grass at Memorial Stadium would be watered by the tears that tumbled at his feet.

So, when his 40 years of coaching officially expired, and the scoreboard clock had nothing left it could give him, Doug Porter said good-bye. He had played and replayed this farewell "millions of times" in his mind, not quite sure how it would finally turn out when the sense of closure enveloped him.

The blocking along his emotional line of scrimmage broke down when he huddled with his players one last time.

"The Fort Valley State team of 1996 always will hold a special place in my heart," he said, his voice cracking. "I will never forget you."

The team recited the Lord's Prayer, and Porter was embraced by players, former players and friends. Behind him, tears streamed down the face of Dathan Wiggins, a bear of an offensive lineman at 265 pounds.

"Oh, I've cried before," Porter said. "Men can cry. I have no problem with crying. I've had happy tears. I've had sad tears."

These were both.

* * * * * * *

Memorial Stadium sits at the corner of Victory Drive, but there was no victory in Doug Porter's corner Saturday afternoon.

In his final game as the Wildcats' coach, he took a young team as far as it could go and finished with a winning season. The Wildcats could have won the Southern Intercollegiate Athletic Conference title had they beaten Albany State on this windswept afternoon.

Porter had dreamed about the Fountain City Classic in his hotel room Friday night. There was no tossing and turnovering in his bed. In his dream, the Wildcats would win either by a field goal or a close play.

Reality met him at the stadium pass gate. The Rams scored two touchdowns before the game was barely three minutes old. Fort Valley never fully recovered, losing 21-7.

"It had to end sometime," Porter said of his 18-year "honeymoon" with the Wildcats. "It's not the way you would have liked, but that's the way life is sometimes."

He vividly remembers losing his first game at Fort Valley State, too, dropping a 14-3 decision to Morehouse on Sept. 15, 1979. He even lost his first game as a head coach in 1961, at Mississippi Vocational College in Itta Bena, Miss., which later became Mississippi Valley, the alma mater of Jerry Rice.

"We played Jackson State," he recalled. "I don't remember the score, but I do remember they had a lot, and we had a few."

Those losses serve as bookends to a storied coaching career that has traversed a playing field spanning five decades. He was a longtime assistant at Grambling under Eddie Robinson, the winningest coach in college football history. He coached Deacon Jones at Mississippi Vocational, tutored Doug Williams, Dwight Scales, Sammy White, Charlie Joiner and James Harris at Grambling, and brought Eddie Anderson, Greg Lloyd and Tyrone Poole through Fort Valley on their way to the NFL.

He battled back from a heart attack in 1985 and prostate cancer 10 years later. He survived. He prospered. Porter filled his career with "enough memories to last a lifetime."

"It's like a quilt," he said. "There are a lot of pieces in the fabric. It's hard to pick out any one patch in that quilt."

In 1954, when he followed his father's footsteps into coaching, he said there were three basic ways for a black man to make it in life.

"You could go into the fight game, like Joe Louis," he said. "If you could sing or dance, you could go into entertainment. Or you could get into education and become a teacher, principal or coach.

"I wasn't good with my fists, and I couldn't sing or dance."

Saturday was his last dance, a slow dance, an emotional one. Doug Porter spent his final afternoon on the sidelines the same way he spent them all—with class. Fort Valley fans could thank him for that. Eighteen seasons ago, he had taken over a troubled program, rocked by the arrest and conviction of a former head coach on theft charges. Porter not only restored dignity to the Wildcats but perpetuated it. He saw his mission as not just producing good football players but good citizens of the world.

"My mother had wanted me to be a doctor," he said. "Doctors save lives. Football coaches save souls."

Souls were saved. Tears were shed. The big man with the big heart walked away and told those around him he was fortunate to have been there for the long ride.

"Get your heads up," running back Terrence Foy shouted to his teammates in the last huddle of the season. "We play for the best football coach in the whole world."

'Wouldn't swap my life with anyone'

April 8, 1997

The most difficult part was keeping it all a secret. How do you stop Mr. Vine-Ingle from finding out he is the guest of honor on opening night?

How do you keep it quiet when hundreds of people show up for barbecue and the man-who-knows-everything isn't supposed to have a clue that he will be the focal point of the ceremonies?

But they managed. Somehow. Call it the first victory of the season.

They took George Jones onto the major-league field that is named for him Monday night and had him take a bow.

There is no real way to show enough gratitude to someone who has poured more than 40 years of his life into the city's second-oldest Little League charter.

They gave him his own special parking place and a fancy chair, one that declared him a Vine-Ingle V.I.P. They also know him well enough to realize he won't sit still for long. There's always something to be done.

Bill Adams, a representative from the mayor's office, issued a proclamation making it "George Jones Day" in Macon. U.S. Rep. Saxby Chambliss ordered a flag to be flown over the U.S. Capitol in honor of Jones. State Rep. David Graves of Macon read a resolution from the Georgia House of Representatives. Included in the resolution was a quote from Jones that has become his anthem: "The greatest thing is not what I've done for these kids—it's what they've done for me."

At age 77, Jones now is convinced it is time to slow down. A little, anyway. After all, he's as old as the dirt out near second base.

This season will be his last as head of Vine-Ingle's Instructional Leagues. It will not, however, be the last of George Jones.

"He's not going to take his hand out as long as he can keep it in there doing something," said his wife, Twila. "And as long as he's interested, and wants to do it, he needs to be involved. Those kids are the love of his life."

He has watched enough fathers and sons come through the program to fill a thousand rosters. He either has built or rebuilt every field at the complex. The late Tom Fontaine was the city's founding father of Little League, but Jones is considered the founding father of girls softball and T-ball in Macon. There's no telling how many lives he's touched.

"For the younger boys, Mr. Jones has always said that the most important experience may not be playing baseball but getting their uniform or making a trip to the concession stand," said Bruce Stanfield, vice-president of Vine-Ingle's pitching machine league. "He wants the boys to be able to ride by the field when they are older and remember they had a good time there."

Monday began just like any other day during baseball season. There were three boxes of jerseys on the dining room table at home. Jones arrived in his red pick-up at the ballfield while the dew was still on the ground, just as he has almost every day since the Eisenhower administration. He gathered equipment, raked the infield and tried to round up some umpires for a late-afternoon practice game.

He once claimed he had "walked on these 25 acres more than I've walked on the rest of Macon." But those steps have been a labor of love. "I wouldn't swap my life with anyone," he said.

Two years ago, his long-time friend and another Vine-Ingle patriarch, Jim Turner, lost a two-year battle with cancer just 10 days after the season opener.

Baseball always has been a part of him. As a child, he would meet his father, who worked for the railroad, every afternoon at 4 p.m. They could be at the ballpark in Central City Park in time for the first pitch at 4:15 p.m.

In high school, he worked as equipment manager for the Mercer football, basketball and baseball teams and later was awarded a scholarship there. In the 1930s, he spent three seasons as trainer, business manager and traveling secretary for the Macon Peaches.

But his life's calling soon became the lure of the Little League field. He got his first coaching assignment by accident. The president of the league called him the night before the season opened in 1958. A manager had quit. Would he take over the team?

Since he retired as a civilian employee at Robins Air Force Base in 1972, his "retirement" has covered nearly all the bases. For years, he has run Vine-Ingle's instructional leagues with a big stick. He once joked that it was a "dictatorship that I try to make look like a democracy." He handpicks his managers, coordinates practices and even has modified rules to make the game more enjoyable for younger children.

"His philosophy always has been that Little League baseball should be fun, and he preaches that every day," said Broadus Marshall, a past president at Vine-Ingle now serving as vice-president for T-ball.

On any spring evening, with a baseball game in his sights, Jones can launch a discussion on everything from the designated hitter to the price of tea in China. Give him the opportunity, and he'll bend your ears so much your cap will fall off.

But Monday, on a night when little kids and big kids put down their barbecue plates long enough to honor him, George Jones was practically speechless.

He smiled. It was a night when everybody smiled back.

Blessings Count More than the Score

Nov. 28, 1996

As we sit down for some generous helpings of turkey and pigskin on the same day, let's remember our blessings count more than the score of some football game.

It is for these things that I am thankful:

For Harley Bowers, who poured 37 years of his life into this newspaper and hasn't slowed down, even in retirement. He always is working to make Macon a better place to live. ...That I did not throw a hanging slider to Jim Leyritz in Game 4 of the World Series. ...That the song "New York, New York" finally has stopped playing in my head. ...

That the Olympics have come and gone, and that we're all better off for them having been. ... For Macon's Mo Leverett, who has dedicated his life to living and working as a missionary and football coach in the toughest inner-city housing project in New Orleans. ...

For the return of the Macon Whoopee, the second-greatest nickname in all of sports behind the Kissimee Astros. ... That Georgia had the good sense to hire Robert Sapp as its baseball coach. ... That the Georgia High School Association will bring all of its basketball tournaments to Macon for our own version of "March Madness." ...

For playing fields where little boys reach back and find the man inside them. For playing fields where grown men reach back and find the little boy inside them. ... For letters that begin with the words: "Mr. Grisamore, thank you for the brilliant. ..." That I was not Greg Norman on the final day at The Masters. ... For hot chocolate at cold football stadiums on Friday nights. ...

For Lars Anderson, who has had the vision to propose a recreation complex and the determination to see that it gets built. ... That John Smoltz is still a Brave, and Jeff George is no longer a Falcon. ... For Becky Brown, the little girl in the soap box derby car who grew up to become a basketball All-American. ...

For the courage of Brett Butler and Evander Holyfield. ... For the Olympic moments we shared with Americus swimmer Angel Martino.

... For the philosophy of Will Rogers, who once said: "Golf is good for the soul. You get so mad at yourself, you forget to hate your enemies." ... That I still have a zero slugging percentage against deer on the highway. I hope to continue as a lifetime .000 hitter. ...

For Mary Holtz, who stayed behind for another year with the Macon Braves. ... For winning the battle of deadline and hitting a huge stretch of green lights on my way to work. ... For the Vine-Ingle Mighty League Marlins, who let me be their coach. I won't ever forget you, guys. ... That my children will not grow up to be a spitting image of Roberto Alomar. ... For Walter Morgan, of Haddock, who didn't take up golf until he was on the back nine of life and won two tournaments on the Senior PGA Tour this year. ... For Macon bobsledder Chip Minton, still out there proving that making the 1994 Olympic team was no fluke. ...

For Atlanta-Fulton County Stadium, where I spent some of the greatest moments of my sports life. Thanks for the memories. ... For Big Bertha, who can be a straight lady when she cooperates. And, on some glorious days on the golf course, she is my No. 2 sweetheart....

For Robert D. Hill, the best Zamboni driver I know. ... For the moment the wheels safely touch down on the runway. ... For a big chew of bubble gum or sunflower seeds. ... For angels in the outfield and infield. ...

For Delinda, Ed, Grant and Jake, who have to be good sports to put up with me. They are gold medalists in my heart.

Happy Thanksgiving.

Part Seven

Some Heroes for Our Times

Helping Hope find Desire

August 25, 1996

Hardly a night passes when the sound of a gun does not wake him.

He lies in bed, wondering where the shot was fired. The next block? No, it was too close. Must have been near the street corner.

As the gangs and dope dealers work overtime in the public housing projects of New Orleans, the cloak of darkness conceals much of their activity.

But Mo Leverett and his wife, Ellen, know they are out there. They can hear them.

When the guns go off, Leverett will get up to check on his three young daughters in their beds.

Although the doors are locked at the small, brick house on Edna Street, there are no guarantees.

His car has been stolen twice. He once rescued a teen-age boy, bleeding from bullet wounds, near the back door. And then there was the time when a stray bullet came through the sliding glass door a few feet from the chair in the living room where Ellen was sitting.

When Leverett was growing up in Macon, about the only sounds he heard at night were the train as it passed beneath the Park Street trestle or a car honking its horn over on Vineville Avenue.

Now, in the city of the Mardi Gras, he listens for the echo of gunfire snapping in the dark, as it has almost every night for the last six years. All that can be done is to hang on until morning, when the sun will come up on Desire, the largest public housing development in the Southeast and one of the most crime-ridden.

Then it will be time for Leverett, a 31-year-old minister, to pour his talent, energy and commitment into the day ahead. He will wear many hats—preacher, football coach, counselor, missionary, mentor, tutor, and musician.

In six years, he is convinced that his urban ministry has saved lives and turned countless others toward the goal line. Still, there is too much crime, too much poverty, too much sadness, too much gunfire piercing the night.

"My goal is to work myself out of a job," Leverett said. "Desire was rated as the worst public housing site in the country by HUD (Department of Housing and Urban Development). It's a rough area. If we can do something that works here, it can work anywhere."

Football gave Mo Leverett a good start in life. He came up through the ranks of the Macon Midget Football Association, played in junior high at Miller Middle School and was the starting punter and kicker at Central High School for three years in the early 1980s.

He was a walk-on at Tennessee-Chattanooga and punted for two years before suffering a career-ending hip injury during winter workouts. He came back to Macon and enrolled at Mercer, where he met his future wife at a Bible study meeting. They celebrated their 10th wedding anniversary this past Friday.

He attended the Reformed Theological Seminary in Jackson, Miss., and served as youth pastor at Mabel White Baptist Church in Macon.

Leverett arrived in New Orleans as quite the accidental tourist. Because he had taken a photography course at Mercer, a friend asked him to take pictures on a trip to the Big Easy.

Instead, he loaded his camera and took a snapshot of his heart. He was captivated by the city's extremes of wealth and poverty, culture and decay. As a Christian singer and songwriter (he recently completed his third album), he even wrote a song.

"The artistic side of me fell in love with one of the most unique cities in the world," he said. "I was enamored. But the missionary side of me also was drawn here. It's a very needy city. New Orleans has been murder capital of the U.S. for three of the last four years. And there are more people living in public housing per capita than anywhere in the country.

"I have seen poverty and some of the most depressed places in the Deep South. I have been through rural and urban Georgia and seen projects and hard neighborhoods. I had friends in Macon who grew up in Stinsonville and Bird City. But I never had seen anything like Desire. It looked like the scene out of a war movie. It looked like you had exited America and entered Beirut or something."

Nobody forced him to move to Desire in 1990, to integrate the neighborhood as its first white family. No one required him to settle in among the ruined houses and ruined lives, where his children, ages 4 years to 2 months, cannot safely play in their own yard.

"It wasn't anybody but God himself, giving me vision and planting a dream in my heart," he said. "We looked at other model programs for urban ministries all over the country, and the most successful aspect of all of them was living in the neighborhood."

So he bought a house caddy-corner to the projects and across from George Washington Carver High School, where he became a volunteer kicking and weight training coach.

He joined the coaching staff at the school just as its most famous player—Indianapolis Colts running back Marshall Faulk—was leaving for college at San Diego State, where he was a three-time All-America selection and finished second in the 1992 Heisman Trophy balloting.

Leverett soon discovered that football was his best outreach program.

"That's my inroad, my ticket into this community," he said. "Everybody knows me as Coach Mo. Coaching at the high school gave me instant credibility. People can identify me with coaching and not as some religious, white do-gooder. It has given me instant access into the lives of young men and women.

"You've got to remember that a lot of these kids have never known a white person, and they obviously were suspicious of a guy coming in from the outside. They were not sure of my motives, and suspected I might be an undercover cop. What's interesting is that, if I had been a cop, I could have arrested every one of them for some crime—from stealing cars to selling drugs. Right after I came, we had a gun incident in the locker room. We used to have to go down to juvenile court at least once a week. Now we don't have to go at all."

That, in itself, is assurance that his efforts—a combination of pizza, hamburgers, basketball and Bible study—are working. He invites youngsters into his home and shows them he cares about them.

He considers his role as somewhat of a "father to the fatherless" because an estimated 98 percent of the young people he works with do not come from "traditional family" homes. He said they need someone to "step into their faces and force them to do right."

He loves to tell the story of a young player a few years ago who was on the fast track to becoming a drug dealer. "His Starter jacket was filled with cocaine, and he had been arrested for car theft," Leverett said. "His grade-point average was zero-something."

With Leverett's help, the young running back raised his grades, passed his college entrance exam on his final try and got a full scholarship to Nevada-Las Vegas. When he graduates, he plans to return to New Orleans to attend law school or to work with Leverett's Desire Street Ministries.

Where will it all lead? It's a long road out of Desire. Leverett said he has pledged to remain for 15 years, so his tenure has not even reached the midfield stripe. By the time he is prepared to leave, his oldest daughter will be ready to start high school.

"If I do my job, we will bring up leaders who have adopted the same vision and will carry it to fruition," he said. "For now, I can see myself being a coach—in so many different ways."

He still has faith there may come a night when he does not wake up to the sound of a gun.

Desire always will be there.

In his own way, he has brought Hope.

Where There's a Wheel, There's a Way

Sept. 5, 1995

The steep hill at St. Paul Apartments traditionally has been the gut check for the annual Labor Day Road Race. Runners groan at the bottom, grimace at its midpoint and raise their clenched fists in victory at the top.

Macon's Glenn Mumford was among those dreading the uphill battle of St. Paul, the monster that grabs racers just past the 4-mile marker of the 10K event. It made him tired just anticipating it.

"The whole race I was thinking about that hill," he said.

The hill poses more problems for Mumford than most, only it does not make him leg-weary. From his wheelchair, he must pull the incline with the torque in his strong arms and shoulders.

Early Monday morning, the 31-year-old never would have guessed his problems actually would begin about 100 yards before he began the ascent at St. Paul. After crossing the bridge at 1-75, his wheelchair veered out of control as it gathered speed downhill.

Witnesses said he crashed going at least 25 mph. Mumford can't really recall.

"It's all a blur," he said. "I was trying to correct my steering when I was going toward the curb. I tried to pull it away but I pulled back. That's what kicked me over."

Bruce Radcliffe, a race volunteer, was escorting Mumford on his bicycle and saw the horrible crash unfold.

"He was going one way and the wheelchair was going the other way," Radcliffe said. "He must have flipped over two or three times. He took the brunt of it with his mouth."

At the finish line, Elizabeth Mumford could sense something was wrong.

Her son, the only wheelchair participant in Monday's race, had been given a 15-minute headstart for the 10K event. His average time on the 6.2-mile course was about 45 minutes. At 8:15, she stared down the forked road at Central City Park.

Where was he?

"I was uneasy because he had been having some problems with hills in his training," she said. "He had a new pillow in his seat."

Quitting never was an option for Glenn Mumford. His mouth was cut and bleeding. When you challenge the pavement with your upper lip, the pavement usually wins.

His arms were scraped. Medical personnel rushed to the scene, but all Mumford needed was a few minutes to compose himself.

"He told us he was going to finish the race before we even asked him," Radcliffe said. After Mumford crossed the finish line to cheering some 89 minutes after his start, Radcliffe would describe the wheelchair race in one word: "Courage."

"There never was any doubt in my mind I was going to finish," Mumford said. "My mouth hurt. My arm burned. But I can take the scratches. I try not to let anything ever stop me."

That's just the way Elizabeth Mumford's son has raced through life. Born with spina bifida, he has never walked.

"He never complains about anything," she said. "People will ask him how he feels when he can't do something, and he always says: 'I don't think about it. I think about the things I can do and forget what I can't do.' That's been his attitude his whole life."

His handicap hasn't stopped him from playing a variety of sports— wheelchair soccer, tennis, bowling and shooting pool.

"He even goes dancing every Saturday night at Chasen's," said his mother. "He dances on the back of his wheels."

Those wheels were slow-dancing as he chugged the hill at St. Paul's after his mishap. Runners gave him encouragement as they passed. Spectators lining the street cheered and clapped as he turned his wheels toward downtown.

At the finish line, he was greeted with an ice bag and a trip to the first-aid tent. A proud mother choked back tears and said what everybody already was feeling.

"He's a real inspiration," she said.

And, by the way, Glenn Mumford won the wheelchair division. Even if there had been competition, there never was any doubt.

Toe Floss and Mr. Double Talk

June 22, 1997

He cannot possibly remember all of their faces. With more than 200 shows a year, there are too many of them.

He lives out of a suitcase, works out of a briefcase and sometimes wakes up in Phoenix or Charlotte and tries to remember where he is and where he is supposed to be next.

"I should check the back of a milk carton," said Durwood Fincher, "to see if I am missing."

No, he cannot remember all the faces. The auditoriums are dark, and the spotlight is on him. But when his "double talk" routine begins to rattle around in their ears, he can hear them.

He first can hear them squirming in their seats, confused by his slurring, whirring nonsense. He can hear them when they finally catch on that he is an impostor, and they begin to warm to his words. He then can hear them slapping their knees and falling in the aisles with laughter.

And sometimes he will joke about his proposal to merge a veterinarian office with a taxidermy shop. The sign out front would say: "Either way, you get your cat back."

He cannot remember all the faces, but he does remember the sweet lady in Boston a few years back. She was one of about 500 employees of a software company who had become the latest victims of the man Allen Funt of "Candid Camera" once dubbed "Mr. Double Talk."

Fincher won't forget her. She was middle-aged and pleasantly plump, and her eyes sparkled when she approached him. She told him he was marvelous.

"Thank you very much," he told her. "It does me a lot of good to make people laugh."

She took him by the shoulders.

"No, Durwood," she said. "You don't make people laugh. You *ALLOW* them to laugh."

* * * * * * *

121

Durwood Fincher has had a long journey since his days growing up in a three-room house in Payne City, a one-time cotton mill village near the Macon neighborhoods of Vineville and Bellevue.

He admittedly has come a long way since his days of teaching school, sleeping on a friend's sofa and having a bank teller once lean over and whisper about the $25 check he was trying to cash: "Mr. Fincher, we don't seem to have enough money in our account."

And Mr. Double Talk has come a long way since achieving a measure of notoriety as the man who invented "Toe Floss," then testing the climate with his double-talk act for any civic club that would have him on their program.

He has done his routine on "Candid Camera" and "America's Funniest Home Videos." He is a member of the prestigious Washington Speakers Bureau, which puts him in the same company as Colin Powell, Margaret Thatcher, Jimmy Carter, Peter Jennings, Dave Barry, Billy Payne, Rick Pitino and Tommy Lasorda.

He once took the stage at the American Dental Association convention in New Orleans and unleashed his repetitive rhetoric in front of 9,000 people. Another time, he interviewed an unsuspecting Vanna White, who stopped him in mid-double talk and asked: "Excuse me, could I please buy a vowel?"

A few years ago, his friend, John Smoltz, convinced him to parade through the Atlanta Braves clubhouse under the guise of a nervous, rookie TV sports reporter. Fincher promptly double talked the likes of Damon Berryhill, Mark Lemke, Bobby Cox and Tom Glavine (who agreed with him 100 percent). General manager John Schuerholz was so amused and confused he asked Fincher: "Are you with the commissioner's office?"

He has tickled the funny bone of corporate America with such lines as "It's not whether you win or lose but how you place the blame" and "You are never completely worthless—you can always serve as a bad example."

He is part-Twain, part-Capote and part-Letterman. And his energetic comedy—the double-talking staccato blend of fresh, clean humor—always comes complete with a nightcap. These nightcaps are the underlying messages about attitude, perseverance and the acquired gift of never taking yourself too seriously. With double talk, you always have to listen between the lines.

Fincher, who now lives in Atlanta, is a 49-year-old, self-made millionaire. He had never flown on an airplane until he was 30 years old. Last month, he qualified as a member of Delta Airline's "Three-Million Mile Club." He has rubbed elbows with Dolly Parton and Lee

Iacocca. But he's also never lost track of every significant step along the way.

"It's the journey that's important, not the destination," he said. "If you don't get it while you're going there, you're going to miss it."

* * * * * * *

He recalls his childhood in Payne City as "some of the sweetest days of my life." He would run down the narrow streets past the rows of shotgun houses. If you lived in the village, your family worked in the mill. Everybody knew everybody. Everybody looked after everybody. "It was full of the kind of wonderful people and rich characters that make you who you are," he said.

He remembers a defining moment in his life while playing a game of "kick the can" with other children one warm summer night. He was hiding in the bushes, thinking not about the moment but his future. Would he remain in the village for the rest of his life? Or would he discover the world beyond the boundaries of the nearby railroad track?

"I remember thinking: I've got to get out and do something. And, whatever I do I want to be good at it," Fincher said. "Then, somebody kicked the can and everyone was free. It was like this harmonic conversion. Boom! It was a sign."

His father left home when he was young, so he grew up with only his mother and brother. His mother, the late Ella Mae Fincher, worked in the mill for 35 years and was the village's social director.

It was in the nearby community center building that Fincher would wander on stage as a young boy, fascinated by the slow pulling of the curtains and dreaming of a life where he could be a part of the opening and closing of them.

At home, he would drape bed sheets over the doors for curtains and pretend it was opening night. He would drive his mother crazy with the plays he would stage in their walk-in pantry. He would watch "The Ed Sullivan Show" on TV and was impressed with a man known as "Professor Backward." The professor practiced what Fincher called "a kind of controlled dyslexia" with the ability to read and pronounce words in reverse.

In 12 years of school, he missed only three days. He got a 13-year perfect attendance pin for Sunday school. "Do you realize that only left me Saturdays to get sick?" he said, laughing.

He graduated from Lanier High, Class of '65, along with the late Sonny Carter, who became an astronaut, and a year behind Blake Clark, who went on to become a nationally known comedian and actor.

Fincher received a scholarship to Georgia Southern, where he studied for a double major in English and speech, and became interested in phonetics with encouragement from a professor. He also was able to get his mother a job on the Statesboro campus as a house mother at Cone and Oliff Halls, where she affectionately became known as Ma Fincher.

Teaching became his passion. He spent five years at Hardaway High School in Columbus, where he taught speech and began developing his double-talking routines as a way to entertain his students and hold their attention.

He considered getting out of teaching when he moved to Atlanta in 1975 and survived by sleeping on a friend's couch. He dreamed of landing a job in advertising, but he had no experience. He also had no money. Once, when the bank informed him of his insufficient funds, he flashed some sufficient humor. "I don't think that's possible," he told them. "I still have a whole pile of checks at the house that I haven't used."

Fincher took a temporary job at Westminster, a prestigious private school in north Atlanta. It ended up being a permanent position. He stayed there for five years, waiting for his big break.

"At night, I would go downtown to hotels and 'join' conventions," he said. "I just went in and crashed their parties. I didn't take anything. Well, ... I might have taken a little roast beef every now and then. In retrospect, what I was doing was helping develop my act. It was a process. If someone would confront me and ask: 'Well, how long have you been with Goodyear?' I would start double talking because I didn't want to lie. Most of them already had a few drinks, and they would just go away."

His biggest break came with his invention of "Toe Floss," which remains a gag gift in novelty stores and airport gift shops. It's amazing how far 5 feet of rope, a little packaging and some imagination can take you. He called it the "financial bridge" that gave him the freedom to cross over into his professional double-talk act. He got the idea for Toe Floss when a letter arrived addressed to him as Furwood Dincher. What a great name for a dentist, he thought, or at least someone who worked in the denture field.

"I was at a party one night and somebody made a comment about sticking their foot in their mouth," he said. "I told them it sounded like they needed some Toe Floss. I went home, got in my hammock, and I swear I heard the angels singing. What a great idea!

"My only disappointment was my friends who whispered: 'What if it fails?' And I would tell them: You don't get it. If I don't try, it already has."

He borrowed money from a student's parents to begin manufacturing the product. Several years and several miles of toe floss later, he would share the same stage for a motivational speech with Iacocca, the retired chairman and CEO of Chrysler Corp.

"He gave the greatest description of failure I've ever heard," Fincher said. "He said it was life's way of showing you how not to do something. That's all it is. It doesn't say anything about quitting. It just tells you not to go down that road again.

"A lot of the groups and companies I speak to now bring me in to break the ice. They are going through changes, like downsizing or mergers. They need me to tell them it's¹ OK to laugh. We're going to make it if we just don't stop."

He polished and perfected his double-talk routine in front of civic clubs and small business groups, often performing for the sake of experience and a cold chicken dinner. He sometimes would receive a $50 honorarium, which he called "more honor than rarium."

His first paid show was for a group of oil company executives at a state lodge outside of Cincinnati in 1978. When Fincher arrived at the airport, he realized he didn't have his driver's license and couldn't rent a car.

"My whole life flashed before my eyes," he said. "Fortunately, I talked the cab company into letting me write a check. They only paid me $150 to do the show. The cab ride was $85 down there and $85 back. It was my first gig, and I already was down 20 bucks. But it was worth it. I was a huge hit. I had them on the floor laughing. That's the night I discovered how much people love the element of surprise."

He has managed to energize and impact his act over the years by getting under the tight skin and stiff collars of such corporate giants as Coca-Cola, AT&T and IBM ("it's not a company, it's a nation"). He advises them to move along and lighten up. "I give them the advice of my grandfather," Fincher said. "Don't ever take life too seriously. If you do, you'll never get out of here alive. That's pretty good advice— up to the end."

From the beginning, his act is a set-up. He is introduced to business groups and conventioneers as his alias, Dr. Robert Payne. The name is a derivative of his childhood years in Payne City. He is identified as a consultant from Washington, D.C. Once the double talking begins, the real show is on the faces of his audience.

"I call it the back-door approach to comedy," he said. "You loosen them up, then it's a litmus test to see who has a good sense of humor. Once you get them laughing, it's a study in group dynamics."

The laughter has not stopped. His sense of humor has not waned. While traveling, he sometimes will kill an hour at the airport by having himself paged. "It keeps things fresh," he said. "Durwood Fincher is not a common name, but a lot of people have seen my show. When I have myself paged to go to a certain gate, someone might recognize the name and go meet me. It's like fishing. You just throw out your line, and sometimes you catch one. I just know that I've gotten four bookings in the last five years that way—about $30,000."

Double talk ain't cheap, you know.

His favorite story to tell audiences is about the time he and a man in a pickup truck were simultaneously pulled over on Peachtree Street for running a red light. When Fincher got out of his car, he realized the man in the truck was fussing at the police officer in sign language. "I said to myself: Durwood, you've got a cop with a bad attitude being cussed out by a deaf man using sign language. That's unusual," Fincher said. "To add to this bizarre setting, you are a professional double-talk artist. It's showtime!"

Despite managing to totally confuse the cop ("I had a home run looking for a ballpark") and baffling his deaf partner in crime ("He was trying to lip-read me while I was double talking") Fincher still received a ticket.

As the officer was driving away, the deaf man motioned for a piece of paper and a pen. Fincher then explained who and what he was. They both laughed.

"If you think this was fun," the deaf man wrote back, "let's go to court."

74 years of swishful thinking

February 19, 1994

On most afternoons, Herman Strickland is a hero in his own backyard.

Bounce. Bounce. Bounce.

Swish.

Bounce. Bounce. Bounce.

Swish.

Every day, he shoots 100 free throws. Some days are better than others. On Monday, he gift-wrapped a valentine to himself by making all 100. He had a terrible cold spell one day before Christmas. Only made 92.

That came dangerously close to his all-time low of 88. Since he started keeping records of his foul-shooting prowess six years ago, Strickland has made 186,632 of 194,300 shots. That's 96 per cent. He once hit 142 straight without missing.

"I'm waiting for the day the NBA wants a designated free-throw shooter," he said, laughing.

Bounce. Bounce. Bounce.

Swish.

To get a sound appreciation of his Wilson basketball trickling through the net, Strickland first must adjust his hearing aid. He is, after all, 74 years old. Still, he has no trouble shooting his age on the goal at the end of his backyard patio. Don't ever get this old man in a shoot-around unless you want to spell H-0-R-S-E.

"There's no real secret to shooting free throws," he said. "You just aim over the front of the rim and keep practicing. I don't think coaches today make players shoot enough of them. When I was in high school, my coach would wear us out in practice, then make us stay until we made a hundred free throws. That's the way to do it."

He picked up a ball, rubbed its grain against his hand and found the seam with his aging fingers. Avoid the backboard. There's too much force. Take aim. That's what you call swishful thinking.

"Someone asked me who chases the ball for me," he said. "I run 'em down myself. If you put the ball in just right, they'll just about come right back to you anyway."

If you really wanted to get technical, you could cite Strickland for a lane violation. His imaginary line is only 14 feet from the basket, a foot short of regulation.

But, at age 74, you make the rules. Besides, 14 feet already pushes him to the brick wall at the house. Another 12 inches backward and he would be forced to shoot hoops from inside his den.

Strickland was a senior citizen before he became versed on the finer points of free-throw shooting. His basketball career never advanced past high school in Northport, Ala.—just across the Black Warrior River from Tuscaloosa—and his coach would make his team shoot underhanded or granny style. So much for tradition and technique.

His first love, when he came to Macon in 1953, was Putt-Putt. He hooked his wife and six children on miniature golf, and went on to finish second in the nationals in Indianapolis in 1964 and third in the world championships in Fayetteville, N. C., in 1971.

But when he moved into his house on Friar Court 12 years ago, he inherited a backyard basketball goal. His affection for shooting free throws grew right along with his garden plot.

Six years ago, he began logging his daily totals, and the calendar hanging from a nail in the utility room soon became an assortment of numbers—97, 94, 100, 93, 98.

"I can usually hit 40 or 50 in a row," he said. "When I get up around a (perfect) 100, I start getting a little tense."

His penchant for record-keeping comes from his love of counting everything from the number of aluminum cans he picks up in his Bloomfield neighborhood to the number of steps he takes on his daily walks at Macon Mall.

The weather is about the only thing that stops him—a heavy rain or a cold snap. But it never *really* stops him. If he has to miss his daily 100 on a Thursday, he'll shoot 200 on Friday. Despite radiation treatments for prostate cancer last year, he never lost his net results.

Maybe that's why the neighborhood children often drop by to watch him shoot.

Bounce. Bounce. Bounce.

Swish.

The sound of play never gets old.

Ed Grisamore

View from a hearse

April 19, 1997

REYNOLDS—Bruce Goddard is not your typical, fourth-generation undertaker who runs two funeral homes, serves as the Taylor County coroner, owns a furniture business and can preach, teach and tickle your funny bone.

He writes a monthly humor column for the Peachland Journal, has his own home page on the world wide web (www.gnat.net~naiason) and traverses the state speaking to civic clubs, church groups, conventions and banquets.

"Because of what I do, and have done all my life, I have made some observations about life," he said. "I call it: `View from a Hearse.'"

There are four views from the hearse:

1. The world ain't going to stop when you die.
2. We all need to lighten up.
3. All of us are going to have trouble in this world.
4. The only worthwhile investments you make in life are the investments you make in people.

"So many of us spin our wheels investing our money in all kinds of things," Goddard said. "When you view life from a hearse, that doesn't make a lot of difference. I have learned from my own message. Death is a terrible thing for any family. But, even in the face of adversity, it's important not to lose your sense of humor. I make that clear to people. If I couldn't see the lighter side of life with what I have to deal with every day, I'd go nuts."

Goddard, 42, has known this was his calling since he was knee-high. His great-grandfather, E.A. Goddard, started the funeral home after moving from Macon in 1866 because he thought Reynolds was on the verge of becoming a "booming city."

"One hundred and thirty one years and a bunch of generations later, Reynolds hasn't grown an iota," Goddard said. "In fact, I'm sure it would be safe to say it has dropped in size a notch or two."

His grandfather, George H. Goddard, died in 1980 at 97 years old. His father, Ed Goddard, died in 1994. It was his father who inspired him to carry on the family tradition at the Goddard Funeral Homes in Reynolds and Roberta.

"My dad taught me everything I know about the funeral business, and it wasn't by standing in front of a chalk board," he said. "It was by watching what he did. Even as a kid, I remember him walking into some of the most difficult situations. A funeral home in a small town is different than in big cities. It's rare that you go to a house, and it not be somebody you've known all your life.

"I saw my father walk into situations that were difficult, and I remember thinking: How in the world does he do that? He had such sensitivity and professionalism. I was attracted to what he was doing."

When he was very young, Goddard can remember his father operating the funeral home out of the back of the family's general store at the corner of Marion and Winston streets in downtown Reynolds.

At Goddard's Store, where Goddard still maintains some office space away from his funeral homes, you could buy "everything from hoop cheese to Evinrude motors." So you could go by to pay your bills, as well as pay your last respects.

"My daddy was the most talented person I've ever met in my life," Goddard said. "He sold groceries, ran a meat market, and was the dealer for Browning Guns and Wilson Sporting Goods. He dug nearly every well in the county. He was a G.E. appliance dealer. He sold and repaired TVs. It was funny. You would go in and get your produce, go by the dairy counter, order a roast, then go in the back past the televisions and appliances to find out who had died.

"I've never seen a funeral home in the back of Wal-Mart or Kroger, but there was one at Goddard's Store. Talk about one-stop shopping!"

Goddard went with his father on his first "death call" when he was 13 years old. While his father met with the family of the man who died, Goddard was instructed to take the stretcher into the house and wait.

"I was in there by myself, and I thought I saw the man who was in the bed move," Goddard said. "My heart dropped into my stomach. I told myself that surely I didn't see that. When I saw him reach up and scratch his nose, I was backing out of there. My father came in and showed me that the dead man was over in a chair. I had been watching his invalid father, who was sleeping. Well, that guy almost got a free ride to the funeral home."

After operating a small-town funeral home for most of the past 20 years, Goddard is convinced he has just about seen and heard it all. His stories range from bed pans to wild ambulance rides to widow's strange requests to telephone conversations.

"Growing up, our lives revolved around the telephone," he said. "We shared the same line at the house as the funeral home. I'd be talking on the phone and my parents would come by and say: 'Get off the phone, Bruce, somebody might be dead.'"

His all-time favorite story took place a few years back when a Macon minister went to preach a funeral in a small south Georgia town in the middle of the summer. When he arrived, the funeral director advised him that the family had made an unusual request.

The family of the woman who had died had remembered that her favorite song was "Jingle Bells" and asked that it be sung at the funeral. The young man who had been asked to sing had gotten together with the pianist and found the music and all the verses.

"So, in the middle of summer in south Georgia, at the appropriate time, the young man started to sing: 'Dashing through the snow, in a one-horse open sleigh. ...' People in the audience were looking down at the floor. Mourners, standing against the walls of the small Baptist church, were trying to cool themselves with the hand-held funeral home fans as he sang. The more he sang, the worse it got. The singer was looking for a hole he could fall in. He finally got through with the song.

"At the cemetery, the funeral director went up and told the young man that a terrible mistake had been made. The song they wanted sung was 'Golden Bells.' ('When They Ring The Golden Bells.') The young man gave up singing at funerals after that. Last word, he was working at a bar in Albany."

When he tells his "View from a Hearse" stories, Goddard said he tries to be particularly sensitive to people, never knowing if they might have recently lost loved ones.

"There is a time to joke and a time to be serious," he said. He gets his undertaker's perspective from one of his favorite scriptures, Proverbs 17:22. "A cheerful heart is good medicine, but a crushed spirit dries up the bones."

"One of the highest privileges I have in life, other than being a husband and father, is carrying on this business my daddy worked his tail off to keep going," Goddard said. "I laugh a lot and enjoy life, but I honestly think I'm also very sensitive to what people are going through. And my messages reinforce themselves. You don't say all that without listening to what you have to say."